Origins of People-to-People Diplomacy, U.S. and Russia, 1917–1957

Although there have been many studies of U.S.–Soviet diplomacy in the twentieth century, most explorations of people-to-people diplomacy begin in the 1980s and to not take into account the early contacts in the revolutionary period and 1920s. This study explores in greater depth the religious figures, radical activists, entrepreneurs, engineers, social workers, and others in both the U.S. and the Soviet Union who reached across the barriers of ideology and culture and history to forge tentative but real human connections in an attempt to further better understanding between the two countries. All of these efforts prefigured the much more heralded "citizen diplomacy" efforts of the 1980s, which helped end the Cold War.

David W. McFadden is Professor of History at Fairfield University, where he has worked since 1990. He specializes in U.S. Foreign Policy and Russian History.

T0352807

Routledge Histories of Central and Eastern Europe

The nations of Central and Eastern Europe experienced a time of momentous change in the period following the Second World War. The vast majority were subject to Communism and central planning while events such as the Hungarian Uprising and Prague Spring stood out as key watershed moments against a distinct social, cultural, and political backcloth. With the fall of the Berlin Wall, German reunification and the break-up of the Soviet Union, changes from the 1990s onwards have also been momentous with countries adjusting to various capitalist realities. The volumes in this series will help shine a light on the experiences of this key geopolitical zone with many lessons to be learned for the future.

The Nation's Gratitude
World War I and Citizenship Rights in Interwar Romania
Maria Bucur

KGB Operations against the USA and Canada in Soviet Ukraine, 1953–1991
Sergei I. Zhuk

Tracing the Atom
Nuclear Legacies in Russia and Central Asia
Edited by Susanne Bauer and Tanja Penter

Origins of People-to-People Diplomacy, U.S. and Russia, 1917–1957
David W. McFadden

For more information about this series, please visit: https://www.routledge.com/Routledge-Histories-of-Central-and-Eastern-Europe/book-series/CEE

Origins of People-to-People Diplomacy, U.S. and Russia, 1917–1957

David W. McFadden

Routledge
Taylor & Francis Group

LONDON AND NEW YORK

First published 2022
by Routledge
4 Park Square, Milton Park, Abingdon, Oxon OX14 4RN

and by Routledge
605 Third Avenue, New York, NY 10158

Routledge is an imprint of the Taylor & Francis Group, an informa business

© 2022 David W. McFadden

British Library Cataloguing-in-Publication Data
A catalogue record for this book is available from the British Library

Library of Congress Cataloging-in-Publication Data
Names: McFadden, David W., author.
Title: Origins of people-to-people diplomacy, U.S. and Russia,
1917–1957 / David W. McFadden.
Description: Abingdon, Oxon ; New York, NY: Routledge, 2023. |
Series: Routledge histories of Central and Eastern Europe |
Includes bibliographical references and index.
Identifiers: LCCN 2022003785 (print) | LCCN 2022003786 (ebook) |
ISBN 9781032042138 (hardback) | ISBN 9781032042169 (paperback) |
ISBN 9781003190967 (ebook)
Subjects: LCSH: United States—Relations—Soviet Union—
Citizen participation. | Soviet Union—Relations—United States—
Citizen participation. | Cultural diplomacy—United States—
History—20th century. | Cultural diplomacy—Soviet Union—
History—20th century. | Cold War.
Classification: LCC E183.8.S65 M3637 2023 (print) |
LCC E183.8.S65 (ebook) | DDC 327.73047—dc23/eng/20220302
LC record available at https://lccn.loc.gov/2022003785
LC ebook record available at https://lccn.loc.gov/2022003786

ISBN: 978-1-032-04213-8 (hbk)
ISBN: 978-1-032-04216-9 (pbk)
ISBN: 978-1-003-19096-7 (ebk)

DOI: 10.4324/9781003190967

Typeset in Times New Roman
by codeMantra

Contents

Introduction

Although there have been many studies of U.S.–Soviet diplomacy in the twentieth century, most explorations of people-to-people diplomacy begin in the 1980s and to not take into account the early contacts in the revolutionary period and 1920s. This study explores in greater depth the religious figures, radical activists, entrepreneurs, engineers, social workers, and others in both the United States and the Soviet Union who reached across the barriers of ideology and culture and history to forge tentative but real human connections in an attempt to further better understanding between the two countries. All of these efforts prefigured the much more heralded "citizen diplomacy" efforts of the 1980s, which helped end the Cold War.

DOI: 10.4324/9781003190967-1

1 Early American Contacts with Soviet Russia

Raymond Robins, chief of the American Red Cross mission to Russia from December 1917 until his departure in mid-May 1918, pursued an extraordinary array of contacts with Bolshevik leaders in his single-minded efforts to establish a modus operandi between the United States and the new Soviet government in opposition to German efforts to penetrate and control Russia. Although other official and semi-official American representatives held discussions with the Bolsheviks during this period, Robins' efforts were the dominant force, and without him very few meetings would have been held. For nearly six months Robins was able to maintain a degree of trust of both the Bolsheviks and the official American community in Petrograd and Moscow. In fact, the diversity of people testifying to his effectiveness and integrity during these months fully supports the considered judgment of Arthur Bullard that Robins was "the most important, the most intelligent, the most single-minded in his patriotism, the most sympathetic to democracy ... [a man] who had done more than any other American to win a little respect for our country." People as diverse in their work and their judgments as Felix Dzerzhinsky, Cornelius Kelleher, Theodore Roosevelt, V. I. Lenin, Leon Trotsky, Arthur Bullard, William V. Judson, and David Francis all affirmed the integrity and intentions of Robins during his time with the Red Cross in Russia, even when they disagreed strongly concerning his objectives, effectiveness, or conclusions about the Bolshevik government.[1]

Robins had unprecedented access to the Bolshevik leaders during much of this time. His interpreter, Alexander Gumberg, was a Russian-American Jew whose brother was a Bolshevik and who knew Trotsky when the latter was working on the Russian paper *Novy Mir* in early 1917 in New York. Gumberg helped Robins get early access to Trotsky and later to Lenin. Once the contact was made and trust developed, Robins had practically carte blanche access to Trotsky

DOI: 10.4324/9781003190967-2

and Lenin. Robins and Gumberg's papers are full of letters and notes from Trotsky and Lenin to Bolshevik functionaries, asking that one or another small favor be done or access granted for Robins or Gumberg. Trotsky also saw that Robins was given access to all of the direct telephone numbers of himself, Lenin, Dzerzhinsky Bonch-Bruyevich, y.k. Peters (Military Revolutionary Committee), and other Bolshevik leaders.[2]

From January to April of 1918, the struggle for a working relationship between the United States and Bolshevik Russia revolved around Raymond Robins and his discussions with Trotsky, Lenin, and other Bolshevik leaders. A comprehensive review of Robins' own writing and those of others about him and an analysis of his actions during those critical six months in Bolshevik Russia underline clearly the broad and fear-reaching goals he pursued in reference to American interests in Soviet Russia. Reestablishment of Russia as a fighting force or, failing that, creation of as many obstacles to German domination of Russia as possible, were clearly uppermost in his mind. As General William V. Judson often reiterated, one of Robins's accomplishments was "to sow dissension between the Germans and the Russians."[3]

Yet to view all of Robins' work in this light is to seriously misunderstand it. It ignores Robins' own fundamental commitments to long-range Soviet–American understanding, and it undervalues several of the broader political and economic initiatives launched by Robins.[4]

As far back as 1897, Robins defined his life by what he called "Christian humanitarianism," or the Christian social gospel. This animated his approach to the Bolsheviks. The Christian commitment never left him. It can be seen vividly in his diary from Russia. Many entries include a partial prayer or reference to "God our Father." Morning entries often began, "Awake with Purpose! To do His Will – to do God's will in the power the Holy Spirit."[5] The two social gospel proponents most important to Robins were Washington Gladden's *Social Salvation* (1902) and Walter Rauschenbusch's *Christianity and the Social Crisis* (1911). As the biographer of robins, Neil Salzman notes, "Robins's unique experience, outlook and charisma allowed him to fashion a message of Christian social responsibility with a practical immediacy that was missing from most social gospel declarations at that time."[6]

Alexander Gumberg's role in the negotiations between Trotsky, Lenin, and Robins has often been overlooked. Robins himself defended Gumberg strongly in his testimony to the Overman Committee, and a recent study by James K. Libby has brought out the details of Gumberg's lifelong commitment to both America and Russia.[7]

Gumberg cannot be fairly categorized as a Bolshevik sympathizer. Rather, he had a deep love for the two countries and two peoples, American and Russian, and devoted his life to bringing them together. As he said in a letter to Governor Goodrich of Indiana in 1921, "my only ambition is to be useful in this tremendous problem of reconciliation between Russia and the rest of the world, particularly the United States."[8]

After Robins' departure in the spring of 1918, another Red Cross representative, Allen Wardwell, pursued an array of contacts with Bolshevik representatives, mostly on behalf of Americans. In August, he made several visits to the office of Jacob Peters, the head of the Moscow office of the committee on counter revolution and a close associate of Felix Dzerzhinsky. He was singularly unsuccessful in his attempts to receive any assurances regarding safety from arrest for any remaining Americans. Wardwell also met regularly with Chicherin, Karakhan, and Yakov Sverdlov. Wardwell's relationship with Sverdlov seemed to be most positive, and he often exchanged information with the Bolshevik commissar regarding conditions for prisoners. By the end of August, all Americans were out of Bolshevik Russia.[9]

No substantial contact between Americans and Bolshevik representatives would occur until the 1919 trip of envoy William C. Bullitt (accompanied by William Pettit and Lincoln Steffens) to Moscow. Bullitt worked out some tentative agreements with Lenin which he took back to Paris (to be rejected summarily by Woodrow Wilson). In the process, both Pettit and Steffens filed accompanying reports on their impressions. Pettit argued in a March 29 memo that he was "firmly convinced that though a majority of the population of Petrograd may not be communist, most of the intelligent citizens realize that there is no other government which can preserve order." He also stressed the friendliness of the people toward the United States, in spite of "our activities during the past 18 months," and he argued that "the United States has the opportunity of demonstrating to the Russian people its friendship and cementing bonds which already exist."[10]

Steffens also reported to Bullitt in a long memo, in which he argued that Lenin and the Bolshevik leadership were interested in making peace.[11]

With the collapse of the Bullitt Mission and the close of the Paris Peace Conference, Lenin and the Bolsheviks intensified their efforts to achieve a breakthrough with the United States. But now they shifted to a concentration on a predominantly economic strategy. Ludwig C.A.K. Martens had been appointed in January 1919 as the representative of the People's Commissariat for Foreign Affairs for the purpose of economic and diplomatic contact in New York. He attempted to present his credentials to the State Department in late March at nearly the time the Bullitt proposals were pending. Following a rebuff by the State Department, Martens devoted almost his entire attention to contacts with American businessmen. Bolshevik attempts to reach the U.S. State Department during the remainder of 1919 and 1920 were limited to occasional press interviews, radio, and written appeals. The waning months of the Wilson administration only strengthened their Bolshevik tendency to emphasize economic approaches, as the Soviets devoted their attention to preparation for what they believed would be a new Republican administration, motivated by the primacy of economic considerations.[12]

Lenin persisted in the belief that some kind of working relationship with the United States could be affected by economic incentives and negotiation. His strategy for a breakthrough with the United States depended on an integration of economic and political approaches designed to exploit every opening and seize any opportunity to break down capitalist and governmental resistance to contacts and weaken the interventionist forces. Although political goals included diplomatic recognition in the long run, in the short run the more pragmatic aims of a working relationship and the reduction of U.S. assistance to counterrevolution predominated. In either case, Lenin believed that economic ties would assist political breakthroughs.[13]

The various Bolshevik efforts to establish serious economic relations with the United States in 1919 and 1920, led by the Martens mission, have often been obscured by the Red Scare and the political climate of this period. This is unfortunate because the careful and persistent contacts and negotiation of Martens, Heller, and Nuorteva conducted with a wide range of American businesses did much to allay the suspicions of at least a sector of American capitalism. They also did much to lay the groundwork for the breakthroughs in Soviet–American trade under the New Economic Policy of the Soviet government.

These discussions also continued the story of the efforts begun by Raymond Robins. Soviets and Americans insisted on pursuing discussion on the spot, whether in Moscow or New York, that put into practical form their belief that a working relationship must be developed between the two countries, regardless of the formal policies of either of their governments.[14]

In summary, the first three years after the Bolshevik Revolution were filled with halting efforts to maintain contact between the United States and Soviet Russia. Although none of these efforts resulted in a clear and uncluttered path toward full or lasting cooperation, this period of mutual exploration, testing, and probing kept open the possibility of constructive dialogue in these years. In fact, a surprising number of agreements were reached between the two sides. These include continued operation of the American Red Cross in Soviet Russia, the transfer of war material from the Russian Army to the American, the sale of strategic supplies of platinum from the Bolsheviks to the United States, the exemption of a number of U.S. corporations from Bolshevik nationalization decrees, soviet agreement to the enlargement of the U.S. consular corps in Russia, and the signing of nearly 100 provisional trade contracts between the Soviet government and American firms.

Even more significant than these agreements were the substantive discussions of political and economic relations which foreshadowed later agreements reached in 1933. Most important is the fact that Americans and Bolsheviks, on behalf of their societies and often their governments, carried on an unprecedented array of interactions at a time of great uncertainty and in the face of official government-to-government hostility. This was on-the-spot diplomacy in Petrograd, Moscow, Stockholm, Paris, and New York. These encounters struggled with problems of military supplies, Red Cross medical aid currency exchange, and contracts for goods. Soviet and American representatives, official and unofficial, talked about the future, often with very poor instructions from their governments. Their attempts to forge agreements for the end of a state of war and the renewal of constructive relationships, both economic and political, laid the groundwork for future diplomatic breakthroughs.[15]

Three years of probing resulted in a considerable body of experience amassed through direct contact between the two countries' representatives, even in the face of mutual denunciations. A remarkable number of American and Soviet representatives insisted on solving, in the most pragmatic fashion, problems between them. In the process they forged constructive personal and governmental relationships. The informality of these contacts and their often unofficial nature should not obscure their very real importance. Far from a state of isolation and complete hostility, U.S.–Bolshevik relations in the Wilson–Lenin years were marked by a considerable degree of mutual accommodation. Proponents of constructive relations in both soviet Russia and the United States succeeded in restoring contact when it was broken and in keeping alive the idea that their opposite number had to be dealt with, even when it was distasteful or flew in the face of popular prejudice.[16]

Notes

1 David McFadden, *Alternative Paths: Soviets and Americans, 1917–1920* (New York: Oxford University Press, 1993), 80.
2 McFadden, 80 2.
3 Judson to Burleson, 4/10/19 as quoted in McFadden, 82.
4 McFadden, 82.
5 Robins Diary, 9/17/17 Raymond Robins Papers as quoted in McFadden, 84.
6 Neil Salzman, *Reform and Revolution: The Life and Times of Raymond Robins* (Kent, OH: Kent State University Press, 1991), 105.
7 McFadden, 89.
8 Gumberg to Goodrich, 5/6/21 Gumberg papers as quoted in McFadden, 89.
9 McFadden, 155.
10 Pettit to Bullitt and Ammission, 3/29/19, Henry White Papers, Library of Congress, as quoted in McFadden, 236.
11 McFadden, 238.
12 This story is told fully in McFadden, 267–293.
13 McFadden, 267–268.
14 McFadden, 293.
15 McFadden, 336–337.
16 McFadden, 339.

2 Quakers and Bolsheviks, 1917–1931

One of the most interesting, and of longest duration, contact between Americans, Russians, and the Bolshevik government is the discussions between American Quakers and numerous local and national Russian government figures in the context of the Russian famine and reconstruction from 1917 to 1931.[1]

Starting in the summer of 1920, American Quakers enjoyed a unique relationship with Bolshevik leaders in the Foreign Ministry and the Ministries of Education, Supply, and Health. Arthur Watts and Anna Haines had negotiated a remarkable series of agreements with Bolshevik authorities in Narkomprod (the People's Commissariat of Food Production) and Tsentrosoyuz (the Central Association of Russian Cooperatives), giving the Quakers unprecedented independence and control. By January 1921, they had authorization to distribute relief supplies from the American Red Cross, the American Relief Administration, and the British Save the Children Fund. By May of 1921 another series of agreements enabled Quakers to distribute food and medicine to all Moscow children's homes. This was capped by Anna Haines' visit to the old headquarters in Buzuluk, where Bolshevik authorities allowed Quakers to expand their relief efforts in the area "beyond the Volga" to combat the fast spreading famine of 1921. All these efforts preceded the Hoover–Gorky agreement of August 1921, and they would stand the Quakers in good stead in coming years.[2]

Following the Riga agreement, the American Friends Service Committee (AFSC) pledged to coordinate its efforts with the American Relief Administration (ARA). But real interaction with Russian officials occurred in Samara, Buzuluk, and at the village level, rather than in Moscow. In July, 1922, when the ARA announced it would terminate its relief efforts, the AFSC was able to negotiate a new, direct agreement with Soviet authorities. In October 1922, Karl Lander, the Soviet liaison with foreign relief organizations, told the Quaker

DOI: 10.4324/9781003190967-3

office in Moscow that the government was determined to shift its focus to "regenerating the ruins industries, raising the productivity of agriculture," and shifting the burden or relief to the Russian people and their central and local governments, but he also welcomed the Quakers' continued work and expressed his hope for a speedy conclusion to negotiations for a new agreement.[3]

The Quakers made a commitment to continue their relief in the Buzuluk district and in Moscow and to expand to a reconstruction phase. This was the most complete and explicit agreement with the Soviet government, setting the pattern for agreements of 1923, 1924, 1925, and 1926. New programs included providing up to 1,000 horses "free of cost" to the peasants, establishing weaving, spinning, and clothing manufacture, and developing hospitals, clinics, and other public health work in the Buzuluk area. The Society of Friends expressed interest "in the promotion of the social and economic welfare and uplifting of the Russian people" and in "supplementary assistance to children homes and hospitals and other medical institutions as well as to the agricultural and rural economy."[4] In exchange, the Soviet government pledged its cooperation in travel, housing, storage, and communications. All relief was to be distributed "without regard to race, religion, or social or political status." And the Society of Friends would have "power to enter into negotiations and to make contracts with local authorities."[5]

In May 1923, AFSC Executive Secretary Wilbur Thomas and his British counterpart, Ruth Fry, visited Russia. They participated in a series of consultations and negotiations that revealed the Bolshevik authorities' high regard for the Quakers. Ruth Fry reported that she asked "quite frankly" whether the Bolsheviks wanted the Friends to continue, "even if the famine were over," and they said "the Quakers ... were the first people they wanted, as they had always trusted them." Olga Kameneva told Fry that "the Quakers were the foreign organization that [the Bolsheviks] most wished to remain." Fry concluded that the continued help of Friends would be really welcome, for "reconstruction. . . rather than emergency relief."[6]

Even amidst the cooperation and goodwill, some problems remained. During 1922–1926 there were many detailed, at times irritating, exchanges with Moscow and Kameneva regarding charges for freight and transport, staff visas, customs duties, tax exemptions for quinine and other medications supplied, and guidelines for importing used clothing and embroidery cotton for the cottage industries. But in almost every case, the problems were resolved in the Quakers' favor.

With few exceptions, throughout the 1922–1926 period problems were resolved through the attention to detail and personal interventions of Olga Kameneva. Relief workers admired the long hours she spent checking on conditions and facilitating the flow of food to children's homes. They relied on her skill in untangling the snarls of red tape which so often undermined the effectiveness of their operations. She intervened in small matters and in large ones, exerting considerable pressure on the Ministry of the Interior for the release of a Quaker doctor needed at a malaria clinic in Buzuluk, or an interpreter needed in Sorochinskoye. At a 1923 Berlin Conference on Foreign Relief, Kameneva called Quaker work the "most effective foreign assistance" that Russia received, and she singled out specific medical and agricultural reconstruction projects for praise than the International Worker Relief Committee.[7]

Nancy Babb's 1921–1927 work in Totskoye remains the best example of cooperation and conflict between Quaker service and local officials. Babb's success relied on her ability to link her reconstruction plans with the ideas of the local government. Starting in the spring of 1922 she saw how exchanging work for food or material goods would promote self-reliance throughout the whole village. On all capital projects, such as buildings Babb offered Quaker support on a 50–50 basis with the local government committee: peasants provided labor, the local government provided construction material and support, and the Quakers provided, money, organization, and materials that couldn't be obtained locally. Undoubtedly, her gigged success in enlightening the cooperation between both peasants and government officials was the construction of the first hospital in the Totskoye area.[8]

What lasting impact did Quaker work in rural Russia in the 1920s have on Russian perceptions of western or Quaker relief? In May 1998, David McFadden and Sergei Nikitin made a pilgrimage to Buzuluk, Totskoye, Sorochinskoye, and Mogotovo. In two weeks they met with 15 survivors of the great famine, in village market places, churches, homes, and other locations, sometimes spontaneously, sometimes on the introduction of acquaintance and friends. Most without exception, these older people not only had vivid memories of the famine and those who brought relief, but they also expressed gratitude for the "Anglo Americans" and often "Kwakeree" or Quakers and their generous deeds.[9]

Notes

1 For the full story, see David McFadden and Claire Gorfinkel, *Constructive Spirit: Quakers in Revolutionary Russia* (Pasadena, CA: Intentional Productions, 2004).

2 McFadden and Gorfinkel, 134.
3 Lander to Norment, December 15, 1922, AFSC archives, quoted in Mc-Fadden and Gorfinkel, 134.
4 Quaker service proposals for 1923, 1924, 1925 and 1926, AFSC archives, in McFadden and Gorfinkel, 135.
5 Agreement between RSFSR and AFSC, 1922, AFSC archives quoted in McFadden and Gorfinkel, 135.
6 Ruth Fry, "Journey to Russia," and "Second Journey to Russia," May 5, 1923 and December 24, 1924, Ruth Fry Papers, Swarthmore Peace Collection, in McFadden and Gorfinkel, 135.
7 see McFadden and Gorfinkel, 136.
8 Nancy Babb to Walter Wildman, February 5, 1923, AFSC personnel files, 1917–1927 quoted in McFadden and Gorfinkel, 140.
9 McFadden and Gorfinkel, 142.

3 Social Gospel Origins

World War I's eruption in Europe in 1914 and the tortuous attempts of the Wilson Administration, first, to remain neutral and then to enlist the American people and particularly Wilson's Democratic, Liberal, and Progressive supporters in a Crusade for Democracy and a "War to End War" also resulted, as many historians have persuasively shown, in a split in the progressive coalition and a wave of pacifist, labor, and radical dissent.

One of the perhaps lesser known and lesser studied results of this outbreak of radical pacifism, it could be argued, was the American pacifist, radical, and religious initiatives and study trips to Russia in the context of war and revolution.

The origins of what later became U.S.–Soviet people-to-people diplomacy are in the founding of the Fellowship of Reconciliation (FOR), the American Friends Service Committee, the International FOR, the International Student Christian Federation, as well as numerous efforts led by intrepid Quakers such as Rufus Jones, Wilbur Thomas, Nancy Babb, Anna Haines, and Esther White and YMCA staffers Paul Anderson and others, and American Protestant Social Evangelists Sherwood Eddy and Kirby Page.

Quasi-diplomatic efforts by American Progressives such as Raymond Robbins and William C. Bullitt are better known, and those of radicals such as John Reed, Louise Bryant, and Lincoln Steffens have been well documented, but the interaction of all these opponents of the Wilson Administration's policies toward Russia and their attempts to engage Russians in all walks of life in order to keep channels of communication, culture, education, and knowledge flowing between the two societies have often been lost in the broader canvas of war, revolution, and civil war.

This effort goes far beyond their contacts with Russian and Soviet government officials but extends deeply and broadly through a wide

DOI: 10.4324/9781003190967-4

swath of Russian educated and to a lesser extent uneducated society – from Russian students in Moscow, St. Petersburg, Perm, Buzuluk, Orenburg, and Kazan to Orthodox priests and seminarians, to arts and intellectuals, peasants and workers.

Any evaluation of this effort should not be limited to their role, important as it was, in bringing about a relaxation of U.S. policy toward the Soviet government in the 1920s and eventual diplomatic recognition in 1933, but rather as the foundation of contacts in both societies that will re-emerge in the 1950s and 1960s to form the basis for the people to people diplomacy of the 1980s, diplomacy which helped to end the Cold War, and work which is very much alive today in efforts to keep Russia and the United States from again sinking into a cold war.

This chapter will explore these trips by American religious activists and pacifists and their origins in the American social gospel tradition, and then attempt to evaluate their impact, both on those who went and on U.S. and Soviet government policy.

In order to clearly understand the motivation and philosophy of those who advocated better understanding between Americans – and the United States – and revolutionary Russia, it is necessary to immerse ourselves, at least in a rudimentary way, in the Protestant Social Gospel tradition, as it emerged in the last decades of the nineteenth century and the early years of the twentieth century. As Robert T. Handy, one of the key historians of this movement, puts it,

> . . . its main emphases can be rather briefly stated. These include a conviction that the social principles of the historical Jesus could serve as reliable guides for both individual and social life in any age. Central to his teachings, so these liberal social Christians believed, was a stress on the immanence of God, the goodness and worth of man, and the coming kingdom of God on earth. Indeed, they affirmed, at the very heart of his gospel wqs the message of the kingdom, which they interpreted as a possibility within history. . . .[1]

Other historians of the Social gospel include Charles Howard Hopkins, Henry F. May, Paul A. Carter Robert M. Miller, and Visser't Hooft.[2]

A number of biographies of the key figures in the social gospel tradition have been written, including several on Rauschenbusch, one on Gladden, and several studies of the writing of Ely, Rauschenbusch, Mathews, and Gladden.[3] In addition, of course, the published writings of Gladden, Ely, Rauschenbusch, Shailer Mathews, and others should be consulted.[4] All of these shed light on the theology, ethics, and social engagement of these foremost practitioners of the social gospel, but none of them are directly concerned with the impact of the social gospel on those who would develop links with revolutionary Russia in the 1920s.

Major proponents of the Social Gospel, which all of our Protestant activists had read and believed in, were Washington Gladden and Walter Rauschenbusch. Gladden was active mostly from the 1870s through the 1890s, and devoted his life to preaching the social gospel. As he put it repeatedly,

> The man who believes in Christ, who has the spirit of Christ in him, who shows in his life the fruits of that spirit, who, denying himself and taking up his cross, is following Christ in toilsome but loving labor for the salvation of men – he is my brother, and nothing will hinder me from offering him the right hand of fellowship . . .[5]

Gladden also preached international understanding. "He believed that the whole world should become one in which the distinctions of caste, the repugnances of race, and the barriers of nationality were broken down."[6]

But the foremost proponent of social Christianity, one whom all others read, studied, and attempted to emulate, was Walter Rauschenbusch, who came into national prominence in 1907 with his *Christianity and the Social Crisis*, to this day excerpted in texts and collections as the best way for students to encounter the social gospel. The basis for Rauschenbusch's theology was his understanding of the Bible, which he rigorously studied and reinterpreted to find a basis for the Christian teaching of a social gospel in his doctrine of the kingdom of God, "which brought together his evangelical concern for individuals and his social vision of a redeemed society."[7]

As Rauschenbusch explained in 1891,

> So Christ's conception of the kingdom of God came to me as a new revelation. Here was the idea and purpose that had dominated the mind of the Master himself. All his teachings center about it. His life was given to it. His death was suffered for it. . . .. When the kingdom of God dominated our landscape. The perspective of life shifted into a new alignment. . . .. The saving of the lost, the teaching of the young, the pastoral care of the poor and frail, the quickening of starved intellects, the study of the bible, church union, political reform, the reorganization of the industrial system,

international peace – it was all covered by the one aim of the reign of God on earth.[8]

Rauschenbusch was trained, as were most of the Social gospel advocates, in the higher biblical criticism and the "search for the historical Jesus" – going right to the gospels and their context rather than biblical commentaries. He urged students to accept the historiographical methods that he had learned in Germany and that were now practiced widely in American universities. The study they undertake, he said,

> must be critical; they must not accept claims about the past without rigorous testing, especially by reference to the sources. And their study must be scientific. It must seek cause and effect connections between earlier and later evens . . . better he believed to combine one's reason processes as a historian with one's faith commitments as a Christian. The spirit of Jesus, he said, is the ultimate test by which every historical personality, institution, or movement must be judged. . .[9]

Rauschenbusch first developed these ideas in a series of weekly Sunday school lessons that he wrote over a two-year period for *The Christian Inquirer*. Starting in December 1888, each of the 87 lessons ran about 2,000 words and exposited an assigned portion of scripture. Especially in his yearlong commentary on the Gospel of Luke, Rauschenbusch showed that a social mission "springs from the heart of Christianity"[10] "In the Bible," said Rauschenbusch,

> one discovers the meaning of the struggles in which the world is engaged. God has responded by sending Jesus to lead a 'revolutionary movement' whose purpose was "to turn things upside down. . . to substitute love for selfishness as the basis for human society. It worked toward the reign of absolute justice on earth. In the end God's rule will be established and the Kingdom will prevail. Meanwhile, the task of Christians is to obey Christ as he asserts god's wil in every realm of life. This is admittedly difficult, for the law of Christ is demanding. Nevertheless, he is Lord and the way of Christian is 'radical obedience to his commands.'"[11]

As he wrote the lessons, Rauschenbusch made little use of Bible commentaries, for they were steeped in the old orthodoxy and seemed irrelevant to contemporary issues. At this time, however, he discovered Leo Tolstoy and read him with great interest. In one of his lessons,

Rauschenbusch noted Tolstoy's lament that the church had softened Christ's commands in the Sermon on the Amount, and he agreed with the Russian seer that those commands are intended for Christians today fully as much as they were for the first-century church.[12]

The key for Rauschenbusch was to focus on the Kingdom of God *in this world.*

> To begin to understand the Kingdom properly, he continued, is to recognize that it reaches both to individuals and the winder society. . . Rauschenbusch contended that when the church places Jesus's teaching about the Kingdom at the center of its faith, it will constitute a historic change comparable to the Reformation of the sixteenth century.[13]

Perhaps in no other context did Rauschenbusch's understanding of the social gospel come alive better than in his *Prayers of the Social Awakening*, published first in 1909 and reprinted many times. As he put it in his introduction,

> ". . . the wrongs and the sufferings of the people and the vision of a righteous and brotherly social life awaken an almost painful compassion and longing and these feelings are more essentially Christian than most of the fears and desires of religion in the past. Social Christianity is adding to the variety of religious experience, and is creating a new type of Christian man who bears a striking family likeness to the Jesus of Galilee. . ..[14]

In "the Social Meaning of the Lord's Prayer," Rauschenbusch wrote,

> its deepest significance for the individual is revealed only when he dedicates his personality to the vaster purposes of the Kingdom of god, and approaches all his personal problems from that point of view. . . when he bade us say 'Our father,' jesus spoke from that consciousness of human solidarity which was a matter of course in all his thinking. . ."[15]

There is no better way to understand the genesis and motivation of this work than to look at some of the key figures involved in it, beginning with the Quakers Rufus Jones, professor of Religion at Haverford College and the first Chairman of the American Friends Service Committee, and Wilbur Thomas, first Executive Secretary of the AFSC.

Jones grew up in a strong Quaker community in rural South China, Maine, under the influence of his Aunt Peace, a pillar of strength not only among Quakers in Maine but also within the larger New England Yearly Meeting of Friends. He was educated first at home and then, at age 16, he obtained a scholarship to Friends Boarding School (now Moses Brown School) in Providence, Rhode Island. From there he went to Haverford College where he graduated in 1885. From Haverford he declined to continue academic work in History at the University of Pennsylvania, but instead took a teaching position at Oakwood Seminary, a Friends Boarding School at Union Springs, New York. Jones believed later that this choice was pivotal: "I knew that, in real fact, I was choosing not so much a piece of work as the *kind of person I was going to be,* and that consciousness dominated the decision. . .."[16]

After a year at Oakwood, Jones, encouraged by family and friends, embarked on a year in Europe, where he not only developed his German and French language skills but most importantly nurtured his contacts with British Friends. He also had what he referred to later as his first mystical experience. *** Describe***

Jones came home from Europe, married another young Quaker teacher at Oakwood, Sallie Coutant, and took a new position as teacher at Oak Grove Seminary in Vassalboro, Maine, ten miles from his home. From here, in 1893, he was asked to take over the editorship of *The Friends Review,* founded in 1847 by Quaker abolitionist Enoch Lewis, which first emerged as the rival to the Orthodox Philadelphia Quaker publication *The Friend,* but by the time Rufus Jones took it over, it too had become a bit staid. Jones was determined to shake it up, and to infuse it with his particular combination of spiritual dynamism and social activism. As he put it in one early editorial, it was the purpose of *The Friends Review,* to "promote in every possible way 'the advance of Christian Truth. . . and to maintain and honour spiritual realities rather than forms and traditions.'"[17]

Rufus Jones's own faith and his own interpretation of faith were shaped in these years not only by teaching and by journalism, and by his own involvement in the struggles of American Quakerism, but also by the trials of his own life. His wife Sallie died of tuberculosis in 1899, their son Lowell of diphtheria at age 11 in 1903, and his best friend and collaborator, British Quaker John Wilhelm Rowntree, of kidney disease in 1905. Out of this crucible of pain and loss Rufus Jones's own faith and mission were first sorely tested and then deepened.

Although there were points in his life where he saw pain and suffering, either personally or in the world, as a sign of the absence of God, repeatedly Jones was able to transcend setbacks and see them as opportunity. He articulated this philosophy in a commencement address that he repeated in different forms in the 1920s and 1930s, calling it "the challenge of the closed door":

> it is that in the process of besieging closed doors and staying there until the doors open that you really build your life. . . . There is not anything worthwhile in this world that ever comes to anybody that you do not achieve and go out yourself and win and wrest from hard and difficult circumstances. . ..[18]

A key always for Rufus Jones was to find, somehow, a way to proceed. It was as if he took the Quaker maxim, "move as the way opens," and changed it to "keep moving *until* the way opens"

Perhaps the clearest articulation of Jones's philosophy comes from a letter of 1911 of which we have only a surviving fragment:

> . . . my own faith has gone through the fire and many of my early faiths have been burned. I have, however, come through with a core of faith which stands firm. I believe we are bound to face the evolutionary concept of life and we are also bound to accept the higher critical attitude toward the bible but I have found my way to a conviction of God as the living spiritual ground of all reality and I have gradually been able to recover a working religion which comforts and sustains me . . ..[19]

Ever the practical idealist, Jones always found a way to keep focused on what could be – what was ahead – and what he believed God called him to do. A credo for his life could be found in his unique conception of Psalm 121: "'I will lift up my eyes to the hills.' Life is settled by what you do with your eyes. What are we looking at?"[20]

Jones always linked his belief in a vibrant spiritual life with the conviction of the importance of political action in the world. He was convinced that a very present awareness of the God within by necessity mandated individual action in the world. As he argued in a commencement address at Moses Brown School in 1919, concerning the emphasis of the Christian Social Gospel movement of which he was a part,

> [it] is an effort to restore the balance, to bring up the other half of the gospel, to complete the circle of Christian activity and to make religion in its practical function as wide and as genuine as life itself. It is obvious to any careful student of the New Testament that the original gospel held both these aims in perfect balance.[21]

In another article in *The American Friend* in 1915, he inserted into the manuscript a handwritten admonition again expressing this fundamental conviction:

> two things are absolutely necessary as conditions of leadership. The Church must have a living present experience of God, and it must be possessed by an overwhelming conviction that it has a definite mission to work out in the world.[22]

Jones's conviction of the twofold nature of Christian faith and the particular responsibility of Friends to take action in the world was given its truest test by the outbreak of the Great War in Europe and its challenge to Friends in the United States. The war presented to Jones another crisis of faith. As he wrote in the fall of 1914, it was "one of those appalling events which test to the bottom our central faith in God, in human goodness, in cosmic rationality and in onward progress."[23]

Jones's test of faith was compounded by his turning 50 (in 1913) and by a serious fall on the ice just before Christmas, 1914, causing a concussion. The combination threw him into depression, from which he was not to emerge until the summer of 1915. He barely was able to keep up with his teaching during the winter and spring, and found "speaking in Meeting. . . . quite impossible."[24]

Only time in Maine finally brought Rufus Jones out of his depression. He and his wife Elizabeth spent several weeks with friends on Mt. Desert and in the midst of a spell of foggy weather, he made the acquaintance of a teacher also on vacation who was doing work on the island's trail system. Rufus began to help him, and in the process found himself rejuvenated. As he later wrote, they found that

> a disastrous forest fire had swept over that region and had blasted the entire mountain side. . . Nature was however doing her best to repair the injury. A green carpet of new blueberry bushes covered the whole region where the fire had gone and the soil was already pushing into life the buried seeds that held in their germs a new forest for a new generation. . ..[25]

From this experience he was able to restore his life and his soul, and even to preach a sermon at the Northeast Harbor Union Church. He resolved to discover "a new faith for this new age . . . With God's help, man could rebuild the broken world. . .". [26]

The first opportunity which came to Rufus Jones to try to develop this new faith and "rebuild the broken world" was to assist in the formation of the American chapter of the FOR, founded in England in 1915. This loosely structured gathering of pacifist, social gospel– minded Christians was exactly the kind of organization beyond the Society of Friends which Jones could believe in, since it combined strong Christian faith with witness and work in the world. He re- mained centrally involved in the Fellowship throughout the War years and into the 1920s, although it took much less of his time once the American Friends Service Committee put its claim on him.[27]

Wilbur Thomas, Rufus Jones's key collaborator and the first Exec- utive Secretary of the AFSC, was born in 1882 into a Quaker family in Indiana, and he earned his BA degree from Friends University in Wichita in 1904. He later earned his Bachelor of Divinity at Yale (1907) and a PhD in Philosophy from Boston University (1914) where he wrote a dissertation on "The Social Service of Quakerism." As pastor of the Boston Monthly Meeting of Friends in Roxbury from 1908 to 1918, he worked to bring that congregation together with Cambridge Friends Meeting. Thomas, like Rufus Jones, was an alumnus of Moses Brown School. The two men had become acquainted through New England Yearly Meeting, and Thomas shared Jones's conviction that cooperat- ing with God was essential as they were going to repair the wreckage of the world. Wilbur Thomas served as AFSC's Executive Secretary from August 1918 until 1929. He was AFSC's principal champion of Russian relief. His priority in the days after the worst of the famine was to com- plete the work that had begun – to work closely with the government, both in the Volga valley and elsewhere, to transform relief into recon- struction. "Steps must be taken" Thomas argued repeatedly,

> to provide the peasant with the means of earning his own living. . . . Animals, seeds, and tools must be made available for the use of village groups. . . . It will take at least five years for these peasants to get back on a self-supporting basis.

Friends had to show that they would stick with the Russian people through this transition. Thomas concluded,

> The Russian people must be made to feel that they belong to the brotherhood of man and that the people in other countries are di- rectly interested in their welfare. . . . . . These Russian people need both food and friendship.[28]

The FOR was born out of the agony of the Great War in Europe. Two men, Friedrich Siegmund-Schultze, pacifist chaplain to the Kai- ser, and Henry Hodgkin, English Quaker, stood together as a peace conference in Cologne fell apart with the declaration of war in August 1914. These two vowed to keep the bonds of love alive in the midst of war. Four months later the FOR formally came into being at Trinity College, Cambridge, with 128 English members. Less than a year later Henry Hodgkin came to the United States, in the fall of 1915, for the formation of the American FOR in Garden City, Long Island.

The key to understanding the Fellowship is found in the second Letter of Paul to the Corinthians, "God was in Christ reconciling the world unto Himself and has given to us the Ministry of Reconciliation." At its most basic, the FOR is "a company of persons who seek, as individuals and as a group, to take their part in the "ministry of reconciliation" between man and man, class and class, nation and nation, believing that all true reconciliation between men to be based upon a reconciliation between man and God."[29]

The principles which the conference agreed to and which have motivated the work of the FOR ever since are as follows:

1 That love, as revealed and interpreted in the life and death of Jesus Christ, involves more than we have yet seen, that it is the only power by which evil can be overcome, and the only sufficient basis for human society;

2 That, in order to establish a world order based on love, it is incumbent upon those who believe in this principle to accept it fully, both for themselves and in their relation to others, and to take the risks involved in doing some in a world which does not yet accept it;

3 That therefore, as Christians, we are forbidden to wage war, and that our loyalty to our country, to humanity, to the Church Universal, and to Jesus Christ our lord and Master calls us instead to a life service for the enthronement of love in personal, social, commercial, and national life;

4 That the power, wisdom, and love of God stretch far beyond the limits of our present experience and that is ever waiting to break forth into human life in new and larger ways;

5 That since God manifests Himself in the world through men and women, we offer ourselves to Him for his redemptive purpose, to be used by Him in whatever way He may reveal to us."[30]

From the beginning, one of the key initiatives of the FOR was "reconciliation trips" – the sending of individuals from one country to meet with those of another with which the first was either at war or seriously estranged. This became a major part of the work of the International FOR from its founding in 1919 at Bilthoven, Holland. In 1921,

International FOR members from various countries in Europe took the message of reconciliation to major German cities. In 1925, FOR sent delegates to the Philippines and Haiti, and in 1926, FOR, with the American Friends Service Committee, organized a delegation to Nicaragua for meetings with representatives of the reels as well as the government. The first delegations to Soviet Russia in the 1920s arose out of this "reconciliation" initiative of the FOR but were organized by Sherwood Eddy and John R. Mott of the YMCA.

When the United States entered the war in the Spring of 1917, Rufus M. Jones was ready to lead American Quakers into new ways of connecting their positive vision of spiritual life with a path of service in the midst of war. Rufus Jones was not able to attend the first meeting of the little group which formed the American Friends Service Committee on April 30, 1917, but it is a mark of the particular esteem in which he was held that he was asked by the group to be their Chairman.

The original organizational arrangements by which the AFSC began its service abroad were complicated and a reflection in part of the different strands of relationships, both among Friends and in the wider society which Rufus Jones and others had been able to develop in the early years of the century. In the beginning, the committee formed almost as an ad hoc Friends group, under the auspices of Young Friends but with representation from Five Years Meeting, Friends General Conference, and Philadelphia Yearly Meeting (Orthodox). Soon this ad hoc structure became an independent board, composed of representatives of the three Friends groups. One of the reasons Rufus Jones was chosen as Chairman was that he hailed from Maine, from a meeting which had never been through the Hicksite-Orthodox split which still plagued Philadelphia Friends. He was originator of the Five Years meeting with strong ties to Midwestern and evangelical Friends and yet he lived in Philadelphia and enjoyed good relations with both FGC and Philadelphia Yearly meeting. Jones's strong ties with British Friends proved an immediate godsend, as did his good and soon to be excellent relations with Herbert Hoover.[31]

Wilbur Thomas, the first Executive Secretary of the American Friends Service Committee and a guiding spirit in its relief work in Russia in the 1920s, laid out a clear focus for the importance of people to work in Soviet Russia in an address to the World Alliance of Churches in its gathering in Cleveland in 1924, entitled "ventures in international friendship":

> The Russian situation likewise presents a wonderful opportunity for cultivating the spirit of good will. The venom of the world is

directed at the Soviet experiment. When an individual or a movement is to be condemned, it is sufficient to hiss the name Bolsheviki. But how is the world to be made a better place in which to live if approximately 200,000,000 people are to be isolated from world affairs and condemned because they do not follow the beaten paths? With the vast amount of latent man=power and wealth, Russia presents great possibilities of good or bad to the world. The treatment that she is receiving and is likely to receive from those of our fellowmen who would exploit her resources and subject her people to economic slavery, is not likely to further the spirit of good will, either in or outside of Russia . . . . It is because of the fact that human beings are of more value than political systems that the Quakers have interested themselves in giving an expression of good will to the people of Russia . . . ."[32]

The International Fellowship of Reconciliation did not become an organization until 1919, following the international Conference at Bilthoven in the Netherlands, attended by Christian pacifists from ten countries, who began the "movement toward a Christian international (deliberately named to counter the socialist international, founded at the same time. This "Christian international" soon became the International Fellowship of Reconciliation. The Bilthoven Conference was called by the FOR of England and the Dutch Brotherhood of Christ. Kees Boeke of Holland and Henry Hodgkin of England were the leading voices and spirits for this movement. The subjects discussed were War, the Social Revolution, Communism, a Confession of Guilt, Living the Christian Life, and Guidance of the Spirit.[33]

The Bilthoven Conference of 1919 was followed by another in July 1920, bringing together some 60 persons from 16 countries, and representing a wide variety of perspectives, traditions, and philosophies. What united them all was their belief that the social problems of the day demanded a social, Christian solution. The call of the conference to all people and nations read as follows:

To All men.
God is our Father, therefore we are all brothers. For us there is one kingdom on earth – the Kingdom of God, and its law is love. Within this kingdom every nation finds its highest glory in bringing of its choicest and best to other nations in joyful service. Let us open our eyes so that we may see this truth. Let all of us who have seen it clasp hands in a solemn vow never more to take up arms against our brothers or to make preparation for war.[34]

Notes

1 Robert T. Handy, ed., *The Social Gospel in America, 1870–1920* (New York: Oxford University Press, 1966), 10.
2 Charles Howard Hopkins, *The Rise of the Social Gospel in American Protestantism* (New Haven, CT: Yale University Press, 1940); Robert M. Miller, *American Protestantism and Social Issues, 1919–1939* (Chapel Hill: The University of North Carolina Press, 1959); Henry F. May, *Protestant Churches and Industrial America* (New York: Harper and Brothers, 1949); Paul A. Carter, *The Decline and Revival of the Social Gospel: Social and Political Liberalism in American Protestant Churches, 1920–1940* (Ithaca, NY: Cornell University Press, 1954); Visser T. Hooft, *The Background of the Social Gospel in America* (Haarlem, Netherlands: H.D. Tjeenk and Zoon, 1928). See also Jacob H Dorn, "The Social Gospel and Socialism: A Comparison of the Thought of Francis Greenwood Peabody, Washington Gladden, and Walter Rauschenbusch," *Church History* 62, No. 1 (March, 1993): 82–100; and Peter J. Frederick, *Knights of the Golden Rule: The Intellectual as Christian Social Reformer in the 1890s* (Lexington: The University Press of Kentucky, 1976).
3 See Dores Sharpe, *Walter Rauschenbusch* (New York: Macmillan, 1942); Paul M. Minus, *Walter Rauschenbusch, American Reformer* (New York: Macmillan, 1988); Christopher Evans, *The Kingdom Is Always but Coming: A Life of Walter Rauschenbusch* (Grand Rapids, MI: Eerdmans, 2004); and Jacob H. Dorn, *Washington Gladden: Prophet of the Social Gospel* (Columbus: Ohio State University Press, 1967).
4 See particularly Richard T. Ely, *Social Aspects of Christianity, and Other Essays* (New York: Thomas Y. Crowell &. Company, 1889); Washington Gladden, *The Church and the Kingdom* (New York: Fleming H. Revell, 1894); Washington Gladden, *The Forks of the Road* (New York: The Macmillan Company, 1916); Walter Rauschenbusch, *Christianity and the Social Crisis* (New York: Macmillan, 1907); Walter Rauschenbusch, *Prayers of the Social Awakening* (Boston, MA: The Pilgrim Press, 1910); Shailer Mathews, *The Social Teaching of Jesus: An Essay in Christian Sociology* (New York: Macmillan, 1897); and Francis Greenwood Peabody, *Jesus Christ and the Social Question: An Examination of the Teaching of Jesus in its Relation to Some of the Problems of Modern Social Life* (New York: Macmillan, 1900).
5 Handy, quoting Gladden, 14.
6 Handy, quoting Gladden, *The Forks of the Road*, 123–124.
7 Handy, 255.
8 Rauschenbusch, *Christianizing the Social Order*, 93 in Handy, 256.
9 Minus, *Rauschenbusch*, 148–149. For background on the search for the "historical Jesus," see particularly Ernest Renan, *The Life of Jesus* (New York: Carleton, 1864); and Albert Schweitzer, *Quest of the Historical Jesus* (New York, 2015). For a superb study of the rie and fall of the "historical Jesus" movement, see David Burns, *The Life and Death of the Radical Historical Jesus* (New York: Oxford University Press, 2013).
10 Minus, 68–69.
11 Ibid., 69.
12 Ibid.

13 Ibid., 89
14 Rauschenbusch, *Prayers of the Social Awakening*, 9–13.
15 Ibid., 15.
16 Rufus M. Jones, *The Trail of Life in College*, 143–144.
17 Jones, *The Trail of Life in the Middle Years*, 36.
18 "The Challenge of the Closed Door," mss, RMJ Papers, Box 53.
19 RMJ to unknown, February 26, 1911, RMJ [apers Box 53].
20 RMJ Diary, September 30, 1923. RMJ Papers, Box 63.
21 RMJ, commencement address, Moses Brown School, June 13, 1919, RMJ Papers, Box 67.
22 RMJ mss insert, "social Service and Field activities," *American Friend,* December 2, 1915, RMJ Papers, Box 67.
23 Editorial, *Present Day Papers*, Vol. I, No. 9 (September, 1914).
24 Mary Hoxie Jones, "Rufus M. Jones," 43.
25 Editorial, *Present Day Papers,* Vol. II, No. 8 (August, 1915).
26 Mary Hoxie Jones, "RMJ", 46–47.
27 For the story of Jones and the early years of the FOR, see files on FOR in the Swarthmore Peace Collection. Jones personal relationship with FOR chairman Henry Hodgkin, an English Quaker, was central. Jones would be instrumental in bringing Hodgkin to be the first Director of the new Quaker Study Center, Pendle Hill, near Haverford, in the late 1920s.
28 Wilbur Thomas Papers, Friends Historical Library, Swarthmore College. For more details on Thomas and Quaker famine relief, see David McFadden and Claire Gorfinkel, *Constructive Spirit: Quakers in Revolutionary Russia* (Pasadena, CA: Intentional Productions, 2004), 53–79.
29 Original founding statement, FOR US, 1915, Swarthmore.
30 Principles agreed to at the conference which gave rise to the Fellowship of Reconciliation (Garden City, NY, November, 1915), FOR archives, Swarthmore Peace Collection.
31 See Mary Hoxie Jones, RMJ, 48–51. RMJ's own story of the first two years of the AFSC, with particular focus on service in France, A Service of Love in Wartime, was published in 1920. For the fullest scholarly account of the formation and early years of the AFSC, see J. William Frost, "Our Deeds Carry Our Message: The Early History of the American Friends Service Committee," *Quaker History* 81, No. 1 (Spring, 1992): 1–51. For the story of the Quaker work in Russia, see David W. McFadden and Claire Gorfinkel, *Constructive Spirit: Quakers in Revolutionary Russia* (Pasadena, CA: Intentional Productions, 2004).
32 Wilbur Thomas, "Ventures in International Friendship," World Alliance of Churches, 1924, Wilbur Thomas private papers.
33 FOR international, correspondence, Swarthmore Peace Archives.
34 "The Christian International," No. 2 (September, 1920), IFOR archives, Swarthmore.

4   YMCA, Fellowship of Reconciliation, and Study Trips

One of the most varied, extensive, but often overlooked American religious organizations making links with Russia was the YMCA. American YMCA staff in Russia in the period 1916–1918 numbered in the hundreds, and a handful of staff remained into the early part of the 1920s.

Our knowledge of their work has been considerably enhanced by Matthew Lee Miller's, *The YMCA and Russian Culture: the Preservation and Expansion of Orthodox Christianity, 1900–1940* (Lexington Books, 2013). Utilizing the considerable archival resources of the Kautz Family YMCA Archives at the University of Minnesota and two underutilized but very rich archival collections in Paris (those of L'Institut de Theologie Orthodoxe Saint-Serge and L'Action Chretienne des Etudiants Russes) plus the Paul Anderson Papers of the University of Illinois (Champaign-Urbana) and supplemented by the considerable printed primary materials documenting the YMCA's work in Russia and with Russians in Europe from the period 1900 to 1940, the author documents in considerable detail the philanthropic work of the Y with Russian students, workers, soldiers, POWs, and intellectuals in imperial, revolutionary, and early Soviet Russia. He also argues, most provocatively, that the YMCA shifted from its original Protestant but nondenominational Christian "mission" stance to one embracing Russian Orthodoxy. In the process the YMCA helped to "preserve" and "expand" Orthodoxy, especially during the Russian Civil War and first emigration.[1]

Perhaps the strongest part of Miller's work, in addition to adding to our knowledge of YMCA work in the revolutionary period, was his examination of an early effort at ecumenical understanding between Orthodoxy and Protestantism. However, on the religious context of the YMCA shift from evangelical to "modernist" Protestantism Miller does not look carefully enough at his own evidence. Here he

DOI: 10.4324/9781003190967-5

underplays the important roles of Methodism, Pentecostalism, and the huge and important role of Evangelical Christian Baptists even under Lenin. It is not a coincidence that Lenin's personal secretary Vladimir Bonch-Bruyevich was a Baptist, nor is it a coincidence that Lenin sided with the Tolstoyans, Baptists, and other "sectarians" as he encouraged the marginalization and persecution of Russian Orthodox believers.

His work is also thin on the Y's work in Russia in 1920. While he mentions Sherwood Eddy's visits (see Chapter 2) in the 1920s, he only deal with the one religious debate of 1926, ignoring the very interesting trip with Reinhold and Richard Niebuhr of 1930.

According to Miller, a total of 343 American men worked with the YMCA in Russia in the period 1900–1940, most of them in the early period and up to 1918, when most were withdrawn.[2] During the war and revolutionary years, these Y workers constituted the largest number of Americans in the country. During the Civil War, the Y shifted its focus to Siberia and the Far East, establishing a "Mayak" in Vladivostok.[3]

The primary YMCA program in Russia was the St. Petersburg "Mayak" which operated from 1900 to 1918. This program focused on working Russians, "the Committee for the Promotion of Moral, Intellectual, and Physical Development of Young Men." The program emphasized sports as a key to personal development. Membership was open to all, but recruitment was done primarily among white-collar middle-class workers.[4]

The membership grew steadily in the pre-war period, culminating by 1918 in 3,800 members, "the largest YMCA in the world outside North America."[5]

Once the YMCA work had been officially closed down by the Bolsheviks, the major work of the Y with Russians shifted to Paris and Berlin and, in the 1930s and beyond, on establishing contacts between Russian Orthodoxy and Christians, particularly Protestants, in the United States.

Paul Anderson was involved in all of these efforts. He built upon his four years in Russia with a lifetime of work bringing Orthodox and American Protestants together.[6]

Perhaps his most significant effort were visits by Anglican and Protestant leaders of the National Council of Churches to Russia in 1945 and corresponding visits of Russian Orthodox leaders to the United States in the same period, and his persistence in bringing Russian Orthodoxy into the World Council of Churches in 1955–57.[7]

The 1955 visit of American church leaders to Moscow was key and involved several days of intense dialogue, including on controversial issues of Korea, disarmament, and religious freedom.[8] Anderson's speech at the final banquet summed up the importance of these meetings:

> Yesterday we were at Zagorsk, where we knelt at the tomb of saint Sergei of Radonezh. In kneeling before him, we were kneeling before the Russian people. This led me to think of the future of our two countries. What will it be like forms grandson and for your grandchildren? It seems to me that it depends on us, the Russian and the American people. If we can continue in friendship then, with the help of God, the future for these children will be peaceful and bright.[9]

Anderson always held that Americans and Russians must possess more than a superficial understanding of the other for the peoples to coexist.[10]

In addition to the major work of the YMCA at the Mayak, in both St. Petersburg and in Vladivostok, the Y had an active ministry among soldiers and captured soldiers and civilians in POW camps. The YMCA was the most active body throughout Europe providing physical, mental, and spiritual assistance to war prisoners. The major work of the Y was in exchanging personal messages and funds from family members to individual prisoners.[11]

The Y shifted its work in Russia among soldiers and POWS to north Russia and Siberia with the American intervention.[12]

The last effort of the YMCA in revolutionary Russia was in the formation and launching of the Russian Student Christian Movement, in both Russia and among émigré Russians. Here, the RSCM worked especially with students who had been alienated from the Russian church, providing small group meetings and leadership conferences. Throughout this work, especially in the revolutionary period, the Y leadership came to the conclusion that the greatest need for Russian students and youth was spiritual.[13]

The major venters for RSCM work were St. Petersburg and Kiev and focused on Bible study, spirituality, and classes in boxing and track and field.[14] In Kiev, the work focused on "student Christian circles." One Russian leader, Vladimir Martsinkovsky, spread the RSCM work to Samara in 1918 and expanded it to include philosophical discussions and debates, some attracting sizeable crowds. One debate between Martsinkovsky and Anatoli Lunacharsky, Lenin's Commissar of Culture, focused on the question of the existence of God. Martsinkovsky was so active that he was arrested in 1921, detained, imprisoned, and subsequently exiled in 1923.[15] Small groups of Russian Christian students remained in Petrograd, Moscow, Kiev, Odessa, and Samara, comprising more than 400 active members, continued throughout the 1920s, despite legal prohibition. As late as 1928, 55 groups remained active.[16]

One of the most interesting Y workers in Russia was Edward Heald, who served from 1916 to 1919. Heald was convinced that "the future happiness of the world might depend upon the ability of Americans and Russians to understand each other."[17] Heald served in Moscow, Kiev, Samara, and Vladivostok, always endeavoring to find out the human stories of those he met and to help them understand Americans. One of the key ways he pursued this was religious discussions with Evangelical Christian Baptists as well as Russian Orthodox believers.[18]

One of Heald's favorite ideas was to establish a "Peoples University," a free, night school for all Russians, to promote international understanding.[19] Although much discussed, it never materialized.

In his rides on the Russian Railroads, Heald always had discussions with whatever Russians he met, such as that with a Russian peasant in a third-class car on the way to Vladivostok, who said to Heald that the peasants wanted neither the Bolsheviks nor the tsar, but the assistance of America to develop the cooperatives.[20]

Heald also had numerous exchanges with Russian Baptists, who inquired as to whether the YMCA workers were baptized, and about the nature of their beliefs. One particular exchange with Kirichenko, the President of the Soldiers Christian society, was particularly striking. Kirichenko wanted Heald to demonstrate that the Y was really a Christian organization. As Heald relates, "he wanted to know what my Christian experience was, and how I was baptized, and what the rules and regulations of the YMCA were along these lines."[21]

Before moving to a discussion of the "study trips" to Russia organized by Sherwood Eddy and Kirby Page, it might do well to focus for a time on the role of Olga Kameneva, the head of the All Union Society for Cultural Ties Abroad (VOKS). Kameneva's conception of the role of VOKS and the other quasi-governmental, quasi-public organizations for interaction with foreigners can be framed as, in the words of Michael David-Fox, "cultural diplomacy of a new type."[22] Kameneva and her supporters in the Bolshevik leadership conceived of the role of foreign intellectuals as crucial to the Soviet state especially in the era of non-recognition – as alternatives to conventional diplomacy. Kameneva was crucial in the development of VOKS from its inception up until 1929, when she was forced to resign her post at a time of widespread ouster of the NEP-era cultural establishment in the party.

Interestingly, in the 1920–1923 period, the crisis of the famine "provide one of the most important contexts out of which the international operations of the Soviet system emerged."[23]

Pomgol and Posledgol, the two commissions on the famine, both had representatives abroad to assist in contacting progressive intelligentsia. "At least some of the two famine committees' personnel later went into cultural diplomacy with Olga Kameneva."[24]

Kameneva later told the story about the way in which international cultural diplomacy was launched, without much initial support from the Party. "In essence, the material side of the cause was founded with bourgeois money: from the leftovers from bourgeois organizations giving aid to the starving . . .."[25]

> Kameneva's understanding of 'kulturnost', however, sheds light on two fundamental principles informing her international activity. On the one hand, the "victories" (zavoevaniia) achieved by Soviet power needed to be propagated as widely as possible, Kameneva relentlessly focused on the political dimensions of her international work and, above all, on securing sympathy for the regime. On the other hand, she consistently expressed the belief that Soviets badly needed a clearer picture of the outside world and especially of the advanced countries of the West.[26]

"An article of faith she was forced repeatedly to defend was her conviction that in international work, a focus on the bourgeois 'intelligentsia' was critical, because it 'created public opinion through the press . . .."[27]

Kameneva was at the center of all cultural exchange from the early 1920s through the mid-1930s. While her work maintained relative autonomy from the party apparatus through the 1920s, in 1935, the committee on Arts Affairs was established by the party to take control of cultural diplomacy. All plans from VOKS had to be submitted to the NKVD (Soviet secret police) for approval.[28]

As Michael David-Fox in his detailed study, "Showcasing the Great Experiment: Cultural Diplomacy and western Visitors to the Soviet Union," 1921–1941, points out, "the list of visitors to the Soviet experiment is a virtual 'who's who' of the international left and intellectuals of the interwar era."[29] During the entire period of the 1920s and early 1930s, VOKS cultivated western intellectuals as an alternative to conventional diplomacy.[30]

Kameneva championed "kulturnost" (culturedness), a combination of literacy and knowledge, hygiene and behavior, and social-political activism.[31] She emphasized both Soviet achievements and western advancement and believed that both would be furthered by greater exchange.[32] As David-Fox argues,

> For Kameneva, the political, ideological, and propagandistic dimensions of her work with foreigners were intertwined with the notion that cultural contacts with the West and general knowledge of the outside world were of intrinsic importance for the young Soviet society.[33]

The range of Kameneva's contacts were truly staggering. More than 100,000 foreign visitors were hosted by VOKS in the interwar years. What united them was not universal praise of the Soviet experiment, but rather a personal interest in their own evaluation of it. VOKS worked to tailor individual itineraries to the interest of the visitor as well as the priorities of the hosts.[34]

VOKS guides regularly wrote reports on the international visitors, and in 1926 published a short-lived journal, *West and East*. Kameneva made her priorities clear. The goal of all of VOKS work was to share the Soviet experience and learn the science, culture, and technology of the bourgeois west.[35]

Margaret Wettlin, in her years in Russia, also worked for VOKs for a time. Her memories as translator at VOKS are instructive. She exposed the KGB infiltration and showed the ways in which the best of the Soviet Union was showcased for foreign visitors.[36]

In addition to the work of VOKS hosting visitors to the USSR, a great deal of energy went into organizing societies in western countries to promote friendship and exchange with the Soviet Union. The American society was organized in 1927 in New York as the American Russian Society for Cultural Relations with Russia. The figures who organized and dominated this society included mainstream liberals, social progressives, academics, and social reformers, including John Dewey, Jane Addams, Lilian Wald, Franz Boaz, and Stuart Chase.[37]

One of the key components of early American "citizen diplomacy" to the young USSR were the "study trips" to Europe and Russia organized by social evangelist and YMCA staffer Sherwood Eddy and his assistant Kirby Page. The origins of these trips came out of discussions at the international pacifist conference at Bilthoven, the Netherlands, in 1919, and further conferences in 1923, 1924, and 1926 in London, Leipzig, and Oberammergau. These study trips began with

Europe only but were extended in 1926 to Russia. They continued up into the early 1930s, enabling numerous Protestant pastors and theologians their first experience with Soviet Russia. Perhaps the most famous and noted trip was that of 1930, which included theologian brothers Reinhold and H. Richard Niebuhr.

Apart from references in Eddy's autobiography, *Eighty Adventurous Years* (New York, 1955) and Page's autobiography, *Kirby Page, Social Evangelist* (New York, 1975), there has been little scholarly examination of these trips or their assessments of life in Soviet Russia. David Caute's *The Fellow Travelers* is heavy on the Stalinist era, and on intellectuals, but its chapter on "conducted tours" says little about American religious leaders.[38] Sylvia R. Margulies' *The Pilgrimage to Russia* (University of Wisconsin, 1968) concentrates heavily on the 1930s and leftist intellectuals. While its focus on the Soviet treatment of foreigners is helpful, it does not examine the Protestant study trips.[39] One of the major scholarly treatments of the entire era, Peter Filene's *Americans and the Soviet Experiment, 1917–1933* (Harvard, 1967), while it covers the Protestant trips, does so cursorily, and notes that "Eddy regarded the Soviet economic and social system as a challenge to the amorality, injustice, and ultimate ineffectuality of American capitalism."[40] Another important article from 1962, "American Travelers to the Soviet Union, 1917–1932: the Formation of a Component of New Deal Ideology," by Lewis S. Feuer, concentrates heavily on intellectuals, journalists, labor leaders, social workers, and engineers and ignores religious leaders altogether.[41]

The latest work on the origins of cultural diplomacy, Michael David-Fox's *Showcasing the great experiment: Cultural Diplomacy and Western Visitors to the Soviet Union, 1921–1941* likewise focuses mostly on leftist intellectuals and devotes little to no attention to Protestant American visitors in the 1920s. The great advantage of David Fox's work is that he plumbed the archives of VOKS, the Soviet commission of foreign visitors, and explored in depth the role of Olga Kameneva.[42]

Sherwood Eddy maintained, from his first visit to Russia in 1910, an abiding interest, making visits in 1910, 1912, 1923, 1926, 1929, and yearly from 1930 to 1939.[43] His memories of his trip in 1912 are particularly important as a basis for his later observations. Though we were not able to secure a large theater, night after night some 400 students crowded into the largest lecture hall available, many of them standing for two hours throughout the lecture. It was a novel experience to conduct meetings with representatives of a hostile government, police, priests, and ecclesiastical authorities of the Orthodox

Church present to scrutinize closely every move we made. . .. We then went to St. Petersburg, where we had opposition from both the Russian church and state. . .. In Moscow we were granted no halls, no permits, no printing privilege, and all meetings were forbidden to us by the Czarist officials. Accordingly we had to conduct our meetings in secret. We obtained two large adjacent student rooms and by standing in the doorway between them we could reach 200 students a night – a hundred crowded together on the floor of each room. . . . At our meetings in Moscow there was a girl, a medical student, who saw the announcement of our lecture on "The Meaning of Life." As she stood sneering before this poster she wondered what the foreign speaker could possibly have to say upon this subject; she then decided to postpone the hour of her death at least until the conclusion of that lecture. While still in Russia I received this letter from her:

"I am a medical student troubled by doubts and passions. I had lost all faith and saw no meaning in life. I decided to put an end to my days by suicide. . . . A life without meaning, without aim, without eternity, with nothing but human pleasures, was disgusting to me. It was then that I saw the notice of your lectures on "the meaning of Life and 'a rational basis for Religion'. I went, and on returning I went to sleep for the first time in two months without thought of suicide. I do not know what the future will be, but now I desire again to live. . .."

As Eddy commented,

> In countless instances we saw God at work among the despairing students and among the young revolutionary students, in spite of the almost insurmountable handicaps of a discredited church and a tyrannical state, which many students considered to be the worst enemies of the people. This was the Czarist "Holy Russia" we knew in 1912.[44]

The influence of the pioneers of the Social Gospel on both Eddy and Page was substantial. As Page recalled his classes in religion at Drake University:

> In sharp contrast was the point of view encountered in classes under New Testament Professor E.E. Stringfellow. Here we were exposed to the attitudes of Walter Rauschenbusch, Washington Gladden, Francis Peabody and other pioneers of the social gospel. The first of the explosive volumes of Rauschenbusch had appeared only four years before I entered Drake.[45]

Page also recalled the idea of working with Sherwood Eddy:

> One afternoon while walking with "Dad Elliott, regional student
> secretary of the Young Men's Christian Association, he asked me,
> "have you ever thought of getting a job with John R. Mott or Sher-
> wood Eddy and traveling over the earth? I had never had such a
> thought, but the suggestion made my mind whirl. Soon I was writ-
> ing to New York about possibilities. Information came that there
> might be an opening as private secretary for Sherwood Eddy.[46]

Kirby Page recalled later the continued development of the idea of
the traveling seminar in his autobiography concerning the Fellowship
for a Christian Social Order (to include pacifists and liberal-minded
Christians who were not pacifists. On May 31, 1921, just prior to sail-
ing for Europe with the first traveling seminar, they met with 25 men
and women from 7 religious denominations. In November 1921, 125
persons from 10 states brought the Fellowship for Christian Social Order into being, which continued, as a major organizing vehicles for
the study seminars, until 1927, when it merged with the Fellowship of
Reconciliation (FOR).[47]

The Fellowship for Christian Social Order, with the assistance of the
YMCA and the FOR, organized study trips to Europe in 1923, 1924,
and 1925, but these did not include Russia. Eddy did participate in a
smaller trip to Russia in 1923, which was his first visit since 1912. In a
long letter to his family, he discussed it in positive terms, noting that

> I criticized the faults of the present government to the bolshevists
> themselves. Many of them were among the most fearless, frank,
> honest, and able men I have ever met. Nowhere on this world jour-
> ney have I received more kindness, courtesy, cooperation, and
> freedom of action.[48]

The first seminar which included Russia was 1926. The International
Fellowship of Reconciliation council meeting on March 6–9 in Leipzig
discussed the problems of Russia and the necessity of including Russia
in future seminars: "The Council while unanimous as to the greatness
of the task awaiting the movement there, felt that at the present time,
nothing practical could be achieved."[49] Nonetheless, the 1926 seminar
did visit Russia. As Kirby Page recounts,

> in 1926 a score of us were able to visit Soviet Russia. Ours was the
> first seminar to have this experience. Nine years after the Revo-
> lution there were few Americans in Russia, so we received much

publicity and aroused considerable curiosity. . . Three members of our party spoke Russian. We visited factories, laboratories, stores, hospitals, rest homes, churches, libraries, schools, prisons, art galleries, and museums.[50]

Sherwood Eddy later recalled the genesis of the 1926 trip:

I did not go to Russia because I had any fondness for Communism but because, from the beginning, the experiment there seemed to be both a warning and a challenge to us. . . . . We had talks with about thirty political leaders, including Chicherin, Minister of Foreign Affairs, and Lunacharsky, Minister of Education. . ..[51]

Eddy expanded on the details of the 1926 trip:

One of the highlights of our visit to Russia in 1926 was a session when we frankly voiced to a group of Russian leaders our major criticisms of what we had seen and heard in the Soviet union. Rudziatak, then head of the railways and a member of the Political Bureau, had told us with keen disappointment of an American businessman who had appeared to be friendly to them while selling his goods who had bitterly criticized their whole regime after he returned to America. It suddenly occurred to me that these leaders might say the same of our entire party, for we were most certainly going to criticize them upon our return tour own country. Accordingly we had an interview with Trotsky's sister, Madam Kameneva, then the head of the Cultural Relations Society, responsible for all foreigners in Russia. I suggested, and she cordially agreed, that we should meet the Soviet leaders for a conference to tell them exactly what we thought of their system. We would state our every criticism or indictment of it, then give them an opportunity to reply and state their side of the case.

So the meeting was arranged. Our party of twenty-four American held a caucus to discuss what appeared to us to be the chief evils or defects in the Soviet system. Four of our number were chosen to present the four principal indictments. These were handed in writing tin advance to the Soviet leaders, and four of their number were chosen to present their point of view. The evils we singled out were: their totalitarian dictatorship with its severe abridgement of liberty; their policy of world revolution by violence; their atheistic opposition to religion; and their ruthless international relationships, which did not encourage cooperation, recognition, loans, concessions, or trade. For four hours we attacked them unsparingly upon these four vulnerable points, and listened to their speakers. Never in any other country or upon any other occasion have I been more brutally frank, more merciless in criticism. Our arguments were received and replied to in the finest spirit. It was one of the most interesting and enlightening discussions I have ever known. The attitude of the Kremlin twenty years ago was very different from what it is today.[52]

Following that four-hour discussion came perhaps the most significant event of the 1926 trip. As Eddy recounts,

I had pointed out to the Soviet leaders that in three cities of Russia, under the unspeakable Czarist regime in 1912, I had been able to give lectures and conduct religious meetings for students. Why then was I not free to do so under the present regime? Why was theirs the only government on earth which laid claim to being civilized, which did not permit public meetings or lectures for students upon the subject of religion? When the editor of the *Godless* magazine rose to replay, he stated that the Soviet constitution, which guaranteed liberty of conscience, did not prohibit our holding such meetings. Whereupon I challenged him to a debate the following Sunday on the subject of religion: "Theism versus, Atheism, Christianity versus Communism." He immediately accepted the challenge and we agreed upon the terms of the debate. There were to be four speakers: two Christians – a Russian friend and myself – and two communists. Each speaker was to be allowed an hour, with questions following. Seats were to be sold and the proceeds were to go to an orphanage.

A large hall was obtained in the city, a notice was put in the papers, and within forty-eight hours every seat was sold. Those of us who were upholding religion expected to meet an audience of atheists and probably go down to a forensic defeat, but in so doing we hoped to open a little wider the door of tolerance and religious liberty. To my surprise, about one-third of the audience were Christians who boldly heckled the Communists speakers, as the atheists heckled me and the Russian Christian who spoke. Some two hundred written questions were handed up to be answered. After five hours the meeting disbanded.

No such discussion with leaders and no debates were permitted three years later or ever again. By that time Russia was in the midst of a prolonged battle between the forces of religion and anti-religion.[53]

Despite the positive report of Sherwood Eddy himself regarding the serious, engaged, and balanced response to the seminar, the correspondent of *Izvestia,* reporting on the event in the August 24, 1926, issue, had another view:

> Hospitality has its obligations. But it seems to me that truth has no less importance than the laws of hospitality. . . it must be said openly that the audience was cheated. They were cheated quite independently as to whether they belonged to this camp or the other. . . . Enough it is to say that the starting point in the religious philosophy of Sherwood Eddy proves to be the doctrine of Herbert Spencer on the "Unknown". . . the address of Mr. Eddy did not satisfy either materialists or idealists. . . in our labor audience he voice of Mr. Eddy spoke to empty air. He was not listened to even by believers. . . for the priest, Father Boboslovsky, speaks much more convincingly. . . His opponents Prof. Reuser said that Mr. Eddy was the best representative of the Anglo-Saxon idealistic intelligentsia. . . There is only one thing our youth can learn from Mr. Eddy and that in the realm of physical culture. Notwithstanding his advanced years (55), Mr. Eddy is strong and young in appearance. . ..[54]

Perhaps Kirby Page's recollections are the best conclusion to this interesting episode:

> A thousand seats were sold and the debate lasted for nearly five hours. In a letter sent home at the time, Sherwood wrote, "This was the first time in nine years such a debate had been held by a foreigner, but I believe it will not be the last. But it was the last. And quickly the time came when a critical session with officials could no longer be held.[55]

Indeed, the hope to continue a yearly trip to Russia in conjunction with the European seminar did not immediately materialize. No trip was taken in 1927 or 1928. The International Fellowship of Reconciliation Council Meeting held in July, 1927, did include a substantial discussion about Russia. As the minutes note,

> relief work is possible, but passports were now exceedingly difficult to obtain and they see nothing we could do as a movement. We had no prophet who could bring us light on the problem. Perhaps it was good to recognize our weaknesses and limitations.

We must get nearer to Communists in our own country and strive for clearer light and more courage in presenting the spiritual commission of Love over against the ism Christian commission.[56]

By 1929, the IFVOPR conference, with 135 persons from 20 countries (none from Russia), included a fervent plea to Fellowship members, urging "a study of Russia and support for efforts to obtain diplomatic recognition," and Sherwood Eddy again took at small group, his first since 1926.[57]

Eddy wrote dozens of personal letters to recruit members of his delegation. In one to Quaker leader Rufus Jones, he laid out his hopes for this part of the seminar:

> We should visit Moscow, Leningrad, and the peasant villages on the Volga. . . We should endeavor to make contact with foreigners as well as Russians and with both friends and foes of the present government. My experience on four previous visits to Russia, under both the Czarist and Communist governments, leads me to believe that we should be left free to make our own investigations, do our own thinking and draw our own conclusions. On our last visit, our unsparing criticism of the present government's policies was welcomed and well received by those in power. I should not suggest visiting any country where we were not able to make an impartial, objective study of the situation . . . .[58]

One of the participants in the 1929 trip was Episcopal clergyman John Nevin Sayre, one of the leaders of the FOR, who made his first visit to Russia since 1913. He wrote a long circular letter about his experiences which included these reflections:

> And what do the people of the cities look like, now that the proletariat has moved in to occupy the seats of the mighty? Well, to the eye of the stranger, the old bourgeoisie is gone – clean gone. . .There is a self-respect and self-reliance in the faces you see in the streets and in the cars. . .We discovered another sign of Russia's fear psychology in the intensified campaign against religion which the Communists and now waging with ruthless force. . . . Ten days in Russia has not been long enough to afford any basis for prophecy or solid ground of judgement, yet it is impossible not to speculate upon what we have seen. . . . Revolutionary Russia is a land of hope because the upheaval has broken the hard crust of many a cruel custom and liberated from the depths new fountains of life. . . . Yet on the other

hand there are signs which suggest that the revolution may possible develop into an extreme tyranny and terror . . . . . .In the Tretykoff (sic) gallery are vivid pictures by Russian masters of the past sufferings of their people. I was shown them be a young Russian girl over whose head the Damocles sword of exile to Siberia was hanging. Some of the paintings depicted the suffering of prison and exile; the girl showed no sign of personal fear or emotional tension, but I could hardly look at the pictures in her presence. "Poor Russia," cried a voice in my heart, "must he travel the Via Dolorosa still further?"[59]

A series of letters home to Reinhold Niebuhr indicates Eddy's conclusions and focus. Referring throughout to Russia as a "land of contradictions," Eddy compared his impressions of 1929 with his first impressions of 1926.

The strange contradiction between their humanitarian ends and their often ruthless means can only be understood in the light of clear realization of their aim. This was the cessation of all exploitation of men by men, by means of the abolition of private property, and the substitution of the common ownership of all means of production, upon an equal basis of social justice. . . Once they were committed to humanitarian aims by means of force let us see what endless contradictions were involved. . . [60]

It was not until 1930 that a major effort bore fruit, with a two-week excursion to Moscow and Leningrad, organized again by Sherwood Eddy, and this time including several high-profile religious leaders, most notable among them the brothers Reinhold and Richard Niebuhr. Richard Niebuhr came away from that experience with a sense of awe and fascination. "The trip to Russia has been one of the events of my life . . . I am somewhat dazed by the whole experience." What excited him most was the extent to which this new nation had committed itself to the idea of equality. . . . and, for the most part, the Orthodox Church "remained a grim reminder of the ignorance and superstition of a czarist past."[61]

His brother Reinhold, however, was not so positive. In a series of articles in the *Christian Century,* he observed that the state-run economy, with its poorly managed factories and queues of people waiting for scarce and shoddy goods, gave one an "impression of inefficiency." He wrote that the class hatred in Russia had a vitality "achieved nowhere" else because of "the bitterness which centuries of oppression distilled in the hearts of peasants and workers." . . . "The Soviet experiment," he concluded, "was no model for the west."[62]

Reinhold was a close friend of Eddy, and Eddy had been trying to recruit him as a participant in the seminars as far back as 1924.[63]

But Niebuhr's assessment was not without its positive sides. As he noted in an article in *the Christian Century* in September, 1930,

> it is obvious that many churches in Moscow are still open. . . while the anti-religious propaganda in schools and clubs is having its effect upon the new generation, it will be long before Russia will become as irreligious as the communists desire. Whether the religion which still flourishes, or rather languishes, is sufficiently vital and creative to adjust itself to a new civilization, is another question. . . . Our group of liberal clergymen feel a little too superior, I think, to these chanting priests. After all the liberal church of America is almost as intimately related to economic reaction as was the Russian church to tsarist oppression. . . Late in the evening we arrived at a little church hidden in an alleyway. Outwardly it seemed as decayed as most of the Moscow churches. . . but this church was different. The interior was graced with many fresh flowers and the place was thronged with worshipers. The priest, who was evidently a man of intelligence, character and refinement, is one of the leaders of a reform movement in the church which is seeking to establish an evangelistic ministry. . . Following the liturgy the priest preached a warm evangelistic sermon . . . Here in a hostile world a man was preaching the word with power and the people heard him gladly. . . . We had seen religion as a living force in Russia. . . .[64]

Another participant in the 1930 trip, my father William McFadden, summed up his own feelings (and that of many others) in a postcard to his parents, "Russia is dirty, poor, but interesting and progressing."[65] William McFadden was one of a number of young pastors (then completing doctoral work at Union Theological Seminary), recruited by Eddy and the FOR to join the trip, in the hope that on his return, he would teach and preach about better relations with Russia. That trip was the beginning of a lifelong commitment to peace and reconciliation on his part. He never forgot his trip to Tolstoy's home in Yasnaya Polyana or his discussions with Tolstoyans about Tolstoy's philosophy of nonviolence, about which he preached on a regular basis.

But how do we measure the impact of these seminars, particularly the Russia seminar? Kirby Page summed it up as follows:

> It is impossible to measure the extent of the influence of these seminars upon the lives of the thousands of men and women who participated in one or more years, practically all of them returning to the United States to speak and lecture and write about their experiences. Most of them have testified that this study trip was one of the high points in their lives. The impact upon Sherwood himself was powerful and continuous.[66]

The group in 1926 issued a report, published in the *New York Times*, which noted that

> the American group entered Russia with open minds, representing many viewpoints, nearly all with deep antipathy to the glaring evils of the Russian system, but at the last meeting held by the group, where nearly all were present, they came to the unanimous conviction that, without in any way committing ourselves to approval of the present system, we should recognize the present Russian government.[67]

Eddy himself, reflecting in 1955 on his experiences, notes that he was

> amazed that we could go back regularly year after year and were allowed so much freedom. Every member of the Seminar knew that he was free to speak his mind when he returned to the United States, and to write as he saw fit. Personally, I never felt any restraint in voicing my convictions about the situation in Russia. I went all over Russia, often without any guide, spy, or official and was allowed great liberty. I sought eagerly to see very possible value and any possible lesson that America might learn from Russia . . ..[68]

If we measure the impact as one life upon another, it becomes incalculable. The great pacifist and labor leader A. J. Muste included Sherwood Eddy along with Rufus Jones as the greatest impacts on his own life. Young pastors like my father, William McFadden, had their lives change. Young Russians like the medical student who met Sherwood Eddy had their first encounters with American Christians.

And the seeds of better American–Soviet relations were planted.

Notes

1 Matthew Lee Miller, *The YMCA and Russian Culture: The Preservation and Expansion of Orthodox Christianity, 1900–1940* (Lanham, MD: Lexington Books, 2013).
2 Miller, 23.
3 Ibid., 24–25.
4 Ibid., 88.
5 Ibid., 98–99.
6 Paul B. Anderson, *NO East or West* (Paris: YMCA Press, 1985), 113–157.
7 Anderson, 128–129.
8 Ibid., 131.
9 Ibid., 136.
10 Miller, 52.
11 Ibid., 119.
12 Ibid., 121.
13 Ibid., 132.
14 Ibid., 134–135.
15 Ibid., 146.
16 Ibid., 149.
17 Edward Heald, *Witness to Revolution: Letters from Russia, 1916–1919* (Kent, MI: Kent State University Press, 1972), xvi.
18 Heald, 162.
19 Ibid., 139–140.
20 Ibid., 225.
21 Ibid., 163.
22 Michael David-Fox, *Showcasing the Great Experiment: Cultural Diplomacy and Western Visitors to the Soviet Union* (New York: Oxford University Press, 2012), 30.
23 David-Fox, 30.
24 Ibid., 33.
25 Ibid., 34.
26 Ibid., 37.
27 Ibid., 37.
28 Clark, 210.
29 David-Fox, 5.
30 Ibid., 8–10, 29.
31 Ibid., 36.
32 Ibid., 37.
33 Ibid.
34 Ibid., 47–48.
35 Ibid., 56.
36 Wettlin, *Fifty Russian Winters* (New York: John Wiley and Sons, 1994), 258–262.
37 Ibid., 86–89.
38 David Caute, *The Fellow Travellers* (New York: Macmillan, 1973), 60–131.
39 Sylvia R. Margulies, *The Pilgrimage to Russia: The Soviet Union and the Treatment of Foreigners, 1924–1937* (Madison: University of Wisconsin Press, 1968).
40 Peter Filene, *Americans and the Soviet Experiment* (Cambridge, MA: Harvard University Press, 1967), 250.

41 Lewis S. Feuer, "American Travelers to the Soviet Union 1917–1932: The Formation of a Component of New Deal Ideology," *American Quarterly* 14, No. 2, Part 1 (Summer, 1962): 119–149.

42 Michael David-Fox, *Showcasing the Great Experiment: Cultural Diplomacy and Western Visitors to the Soviet Union, 1921–1941* (Oxford: Oxford University Press, 2012).

43 Eddy, *Eighty Adbventurous Years*, 134.

44 Ibid., 83–86.

45 Harold E. Fey, ed., *Kirby Page: Social Evangelist: The Autobiography of a 20th Century Prophet for Peace* (New York: Fellowship Press, 1975), 16–17.

46 Fey, *Kirby Page*, 23.

47 Ibid., 99–100.

48 Eddy to Mother and Brewer, September 12, 1923, George Sherwood Eddy Papers, Yale Divinity School.

49 Minutes, IFOR Council Meeting, March 6–9, 1926, FOR papers Swarthmore.

50 Page, 40.

51 Eddy, *Eighty Adventurous Years*, 135–136.

52 Ibid., 138–140. See also Eddy's letter to his family, September 14, 1926, Eddy Papers, Yale Divinity School.

53 Ibid., 140–141.

54 A. Startchakoff, "Mr. Sherwood Eddy and His Sermon", translated by Dorice White, *Izvestia,* August 24, 1926, AFSC, Executive Files Secretary Correspondence, 1926.

55 Kirby Page, *Notes on Russia Seminar*, Kirby Page Papers, Claremont.

56 IFOR minutes of council meeting, July 25–31, 1927, FOR papers.

57 IFOR minutes of council meeting, August 2–9, 1929, FOR papers.

58 Sherwood Eddy to Rufus Jones, December 31, 1928, RMJ Papers, Haverford College.

59 JN Sayre, "Russia: An Inside View", September 1, 1929, FOR papers 1929.

60 Sherwood Eddy to Reinhold Niebuhr, September 15, 1929, Reinhold Niebuhr papers, Library of Congress.

61 H. Richard Niebuhr, "Some Observations on Russia," *Evangelical Herald* 29 (October, 1930), 795–796. See also Jon Diefenthaler, *H. Richard Niebuhr: A Lifetime of Reflections on the Church and the World* (Macon, GA: Mercer University Press, 1986).

62 Charles C. Brown, *Niebuhr and His Age: Reinhold Niebuhr's Prophetic Role in the Twentieth Century* (Philadelphia, PA: Trinity Press, 1992), 42–43.

63 Kirby Page to Sherwood Eddy, February 21, 1924, Page Papers, Claremont.

64 Reinhold Niebuhr, "The Church in Russia," *Christian Century* September 24, 1930. See also Henry B. Clark, *Serenity, Courage, and Wisdom: The Enduring Legacy of Reinhold Niebuhr* (Cleveland, OH: The Pilgrim Press, 1994).

65 William McFadden to Paul McFadden, September 1930, McFadden papers.

66 Kirby Page, mss on recollections on European seminars, Kirby Page Papers, Claremont Theological Seminary.

67 Sherwood Eddy Commission report on Soiet Russia, *New York Times Current History*, 25 (November 1926), 190–196 in Goldberg, Vol. 2, 387–389.

68 Eddy, *Eighty Adventurous Years*, 140.

5   The 1930s

Fellow Travelers, Social Workers, Entrepreneurs, and Engineers

The aftermath of the religious study trips of the 1920s unleashed a wide array of American visitors to the Soviet Union, driven by sympathy, curiosity, and desire to explore this "utopia" and in the process to build support for U.S. recognition of the USSR.

A good example of these "romantic revolutionaries" was Lincoln Steffens. Steffens, the radical journalist, visited Russia in 1923 and wrote extensively of his experiences. As he wrote,

> there is no doubt in my mind about the vigor of Russia. . .Russia is beginning to live bravely and to smile. But the surest light ahead is the youth of Russia, the boys and girls from sixteen to twenty-eight. They are the proudest human beings you ever saw. They fear nothing, neither the foreign foe, nor their own police; not even the Soviet government can cow them.[1]

As Lewis Feuer has pointed out, there have been several different waves of American travelers to the Soviet Union. The first were "romantic revolutionaries," in the immediate aftermath of the Bolshevik Revolution, but these were soon succeeded, following the relief personnel of the early 1920s, by "an ever growing procession of social workers, artists, labor leaders, educators, social scientists, businessmen, and representatives of ethnic minorities."[2] In the early 1930s, more than 1,000 American engineers enlisted in the first five-year plan.

An interesting contribution to the motivation of all of these Americans in the late 1920s and early 1930s was the fact of the deepening American depression. The Soviet effort to build a different model society attracted all kinds of Americans determined to build "a new world."[3]

DOI: 10.4324/9781003190967-6

A very interesting example of these

> romantic revolutionaries in the 1930s and 1940s was Margaret Wettlin, who first went to Russia in 1932, fell in love, married Russian theatre director Andrei Efrimov, raised two children, and stayed in Russia until the 1970s. Her story is told in the fascinating account, *Fifty Russian Winters* (New York: John Wiley and Sons, 1994).[4] Some of her most notable interactions with Russian citizens were in the 1930s and 1940s. As she remembered of the 1930s: (I). . . witnessed the end of an extraordinary period of creative activity animated by revolutionary fervor. It was not a halcyon period; far from it. But its turbulence was caused by the conflict of the new and the old, a conflict that lent excitement to the daily experience and conferred a sense of participation in history-making.[5]

Wettlin taught English to Russians, and in the process exchanged all kinds of information about daily life. One of her students in particular was revealing. Although she said that she avoided speaking about life in Russia, her own life told much. "Life is hard" was her only comment.

> Her experience of present hardship was always offset by memories of the Civil War when in her native town of Kiev she had witnessed murder and plunder and rape. Now that is over. Now we think about the future. . . . But I have a strange feeling. I feel I will not live to see it.[6]

Wettlin returned to her home in Philadelphia for a time in 1936 and spent several months lecturing about Russia and America. My life in Russia,

> she noted, had shown me how badly that country was in need of some of the things America had produced and how seriously she was handicapped by not having those things. And I also knew that Russia had achieved things that I believed America must adopt if she was to be in actual fact the home of the free.[7]
>
> My life it seemed was taking purposeful shape. I was in the unique position of being an integral part of two entirely different worlds, worlds that not only had no understanding of each other, but had the most distorted conceptions. . .l. Could I, if only in a small way, help Americans and Russians to understand and help each other? It looked as if I was being given the opportunity to do so.[8]

"The social scientists found themselves singularly at home in a society which was guided by fellow social scientists who aimed to build a rational, planned world."[9]

Probably the most influential series of articles by an American on the Soviet Union were those by John Dewey in the New Republic in 1928. The foremost figure in American pragmatic thought found almost the fulfillment of his philosophic hopes in the Soviet experiment.[10]

Social welfare advocates also flocked to the Soviet Union: Jane Addams, Lillian Wald, and others. Jane Addams called the Russian Revolution, "the greatest social experiment in history."[11] Social workers became some of the foremost observers and promoters of the soviet model. Peace activist and social worker Muriel Lester was particularly struck by her visit to the Soviet Union in 1927. She visited churches and the Museum of Atheism and had many discussions with Russians about religion. After explaining her own Quaker views to an Orthodox believer, the Russian said "that's a new religion."[12] Finally, after another encounter, "this personal method is, in my opinion, the only way in which the world will gain peace."[13]

Another interesting exchange on religious questions was Quaker Gilbert McMaster's 1930 visit with a group of Tolstoyans in Moscow. As he recounted,

> The meeting with these friends was a. very touching one and it was an experience from which I will carry in my memory as long as I live. . . After a while one of the young men from the Stalingrad group began to speak and told us of their difficulties about the mission which lay before them. Afterward I spoke to them and as best as I could brought a message of sympathy and understanding to them. This moved them very deeply. The one who answered in fact was so moved that for a time he could not speak. The thought that there were those in other countries who felt and believed in many ways as they did and who were in sympathy with them was to them very dear.[14]

Although the "official" Quaker presence in Russia that focused on the Quaker Centre in Moscow following famine relief ended in 1931 with the failure of a renewal of the lease, several individual Quakers continued their work in the 1930s. Arthur Watts, who pioneered in relief in 1921, worked as a construction engineer under the Soviet government. He first built a steam plant and then homes for workers. He then was head engineer for the construction of a steel foundry. He continued living and working in Russia until his death.[15]

Two other American Friends, Harry Timbres and Rebecca Janney, who had worked in relief in both Poland and Russia in the 1920s (married in 1922), were determined to return to assist in fighting disease. Harry Timbres returned to the United States, completed medical school, and returned to Russia in 1936, in the Mariinskii republic on an anti-malaria campaign. Over the course of one year, they made many friends and healed many. As Rebecca Timbres said, "The Russians have accepted us wholeheartedly and confidently into their lives and problems, and have given us positions of responsibility."[16] Sadly within the year, Harry Timbres came down with typhus and died. He was buried near the Volga in Kazan.[17]

Another AFSC official, this time AFSC Executive Secretary Clarence Pickett, also visited the Soviet Union in 1930. He visited with Soviet officials, attended both a Russian Orthodox service and a Baptist service in Moscow, as well as the small meeting for worship at the Quaker Centre. He also consulted with the staff at the Quaker Centre concerning their work, which was dwindling. As he noted, "personal contacts seemed to be about all the center was doing. Yet these were very important."[18]

And Pickett was never to abandon these efforts at personal connections on behalf of better Russian–American relations. He pursued these efforts tirelessly in the late 1940s and early 1950s. Notable was a meeting he had in early 1948 with Andrei Gromyko, then Soviet Ambassador to the United Nations. This meeting was the result of an encounter between the two at a November 1947 celebration of the Russian revolution which Pickett had attended. At the February 1948 meeting between the two, Pickett submitted his proposal for a conference in Europe bringing together American and Russian religious leaders as well as cultural and scientific figures to determine how personal contacts could contribute to better relations. While this conference was never held, it paved the way for a series of AFSC East-West seminars that would flourish in the 1960s and 1970s. Nothing was more important to Clarence Pickett than personal connections to build political relations.[19]

The Quaker approach to peacemaking was always rooted in people-to-people connections. As Irwin Abrams noted after the Moscow Youth Forum of 1961,

> The soviet approach to peacemaking. . . was very different from the quaker approach. While the Quaker aim was to promote peace through mutual understanding between peoples, its 'soviet partners believed that true peace could only come about through the

inevitable victory of communism. . .Despite this difference between the Quakers and the CYO (Communist Youth Organization), the AFSC participation in the forum did help maintain the relationship, and launched a series of reciprocal seminars which lasted through the Sixties and Seventies.[20]

African-Americans, notably W.E.B. Dubois, were struck by Soviet openness.

Soviet Russia was perceived by the black community in the United States as a "red Mecca" of equality, not because of the ideology of the Soviet state, but rather due to the image of a "multi-ethnic Soviet Union marching towards a communist paradise."

Dubois visited the Soviet Union in 1926, 1936, 1949, and 1958. Over the years, he was more and more impressed with the progress of its people toward a truly egalitarian society. As Dubois said later in his autobiography, "What I saw in the Soviet Union was more than triumph in physics; it was the growth of a nation's soul, the confidence of a great people in its plan and future."[21] In 1958, he had the opportunity of a meeting with Nikita Khrushchev, and he ended his time in Moscow with these thoughts about America and Russia:

> . . .we have begun to recognize the soviet socialist Republic as giving its people the best education of any in the world, of excelling in science, and organizing industry to its highest levels. Our increasing number of visitors to Russia see a contented people who do not hate the United States, but fear its war-making, and are eager to cooperate with us. From such a nation we can learn.[22]

Another prominent African-American visitor to the Soviet Union was Langston Hughes, who toured with a group in 1932. They also visited Soviet Central Asia.[23]

The American singer and actor Paul Robeson took the first of several trips to the Soviet Union, sponsored by Eisenstein, in 1934. Eisenstein had been impressed by Robeson in the title role of The Emperor Jones and wanted him to play the rebel leader in Eisenstein's film on the Haitian independence movement.[24] Robeson became emotionally identified with the Soviet Union. He was moved by his sense of a society free of racism. His visits "made him feel at home." And he welcomed the Soviet internationalism. Robeson was so enamored with the Soviets and the Russians that he became fluent in Russian and a great publicist for Pushkin, as well as Russian folk culture.[25]

But it was American engineers in the early 1930s, by their participation as well as their observation, who really helped to BUILD this new society. They were impressed by soviet experimentation, and by the scale of the work, but the managerial idealism and the work ethic found in the soviet industry. The American engineers were the most accurate observers of Soviet reality because they were participant observers.

A good example of the "participant observer" can be found in the experience of Zara Witkin. Witkin, an experienced engineer, probably had greater access and a greater variety of top assignments in Russia than any other western specialist. Not only was he employed in his specialty, pre-fabricated housing construction, but he worked on the construction of airplane factories, power plants, textile plants, and transportation facilities. He was variously employed by several construction trusts, the Commissariat of Heavy Industry, the workers and Peasants Inspectorate, the Council on Labor and defense, and even the OGPU – probably the only foreigner ever so employed. But it was perhaps his assignment to draw up plans for the nationalization of the entire construction industry, and his participation in the design and evaluation of the second five-year plan, that gave Witkin his greatest access to Party and Secret Police operations, and from which he provides his most interesting observations.[26]

Witkin went to Russia in 1932 because, as he put it "the abstract dream had become a problem in building and I therefore felt I had a special contribution to make."[27] Witkin's experience on the whole is one of determination and frustration, rather than disillusionment. He saw his fight as one "against bureaucracy" to build a better society; he battled against incompetence, corruption, and political opposition and always maintained his faith in the Russian people and the socialist ideal.[28]

Entrepreneurs

On the heels of the adventurers of fellow travelers, social workers, and engineers came the businessmen, determined to open up commercial ties in the absence of diplomatic relations. As Joan Hoff Wilson has pointed out, the various American businessmen who explored commercial opportunities in the Soviet Union in the 1920s were divided on the question of recognition. Some favored, but most opposed, content to advocate opening of trade and the end of trade barriers.[29]

Three major figures: Armand Hammer, Averill Harriman, and Henry Ford, exemplify U.S. capitalist desire to make a profit in Russia.

Armand Hammer

Armand Hammer's father, Julius, was born in Russia and was a communist party activist and supporter of Ludwig Martens' Russia bureau in 1919 as it worked to get American firms interested in trade with the young Soviet Union. Julius Hammer's major goods sold to Russia were medicines and medical supplies, sent through the family business, Allied Drug and Chemical Corporation.[30]

Hammer remembered how he first became interested in Russia. It was in 1921 during the famine:

> the news of that year's appalling famine in Russia had just startled the world. . . . It was unmistakably true that hundreds of thousands of famine refugees were streaming into the Volga towns from their fields burned barren by eight weeks of drought and that an epidemic of typhus was running through this multitude. . .Reading one such newspaper report, I had the thought which was to be the most important of my young life and the turning point of my life as a whole . . . I would go to 'Russia. From the surplus stores department of the War Department, I bought an entire field hospital. . .I intended to present it to the Soviets as a gift and that's what I did. . .[31]

Hammer first went to the Soviet Union in 1921 to explore future business with Soviet officials and to try to collect the $150,000 that the Soviet government owed the Hammer family for supplies and oil drilling equipment.[32] Hammer was able to obtain a one-hour interview with Lenin, who was grateful for the humanitarian assistance but told Hammer, "what we really need is American capital and technical aid."[33] As a result of this meeting, Hammer obtained the first American concession in Russia, for his asbestos mine in the Urals.[34]

He also remembered well his talk with Lenin: "to talk with Lenin was like talking with a trusted friend, a friend who understood. His infectious smile and colloquial speech, his sincerity and natural ways, put me completely at my ease."[35]

Hammer also persuaded Henry Ford in 1922 to work with him to facilitate a sale of 25,000 Fordson tractors to Soviet Russia. The New Economic Policy emphasized agricultural modernization, and soon Ford became a major Hammer client. Soon Hammer signed other major firms, including Union twist Drill, American Tool Works, U.S. Machine Company, Allis Chalmers, U.S. Rubber, Parker Pens, and Underwood Typewriter Company. To take charge of all these orders, Hammer established the Allied American Corporation, or Alamerico, which quickly became the largest American company dealing with Soviet Russia.[36]

In 1925, Hammer established a pencil factory, which proved to be one of the most successful of his enterprises in the Soviet Union. Before this pencil factory was opened, most of the pencils in Russia were imported from Germany. Eventually Hammer opened five pencil factories in Russia, employing over 2,000 people and producing upwards of 72 million pencils and an equivalent number of steel pens per year. Economies of scale enabled them to drop the price from 50 cents to 5 cents per pencil by 1929.[37]

Over the years, Hammer would meet with every Russian leader from Lenin to Gorbachev. A notable meeting with Khrushchev in 1961 in which he told Khrushchev that there should be "more cultural exchanges between our two countries" and made the same suggestion I had previously made to Mikoyan regarding increases in tourist trade by both countries and the desirability of an art exchange.[38] This idea, first broached to Khrushchev, became a reality during the Brezhnev era, with Hammer's connections to Yekaterina Furtseva. Hammer facilitated an exhibition of Grandma Moses's art to the Pushkin Museum in 1964. The Soviets reciprocated with an exhibition of Pavel Korin's work at the Hammer galleries in 1965.[39] This was just the beginning of a whole range of art exchanges facilitated by Hammer from the late 1960s well into the 1980s. The Soviet leader most compatible with Hammer was Leonid Brezhnev. The two developed numerous business concessions, exchanges, and also discussed arms control and people-to-people exchanges.[40]

Perhaps the most noteworthy endeavor of Armand Hammer occurred late in his life. The Chernobyl nuclear disaster, in 1986, brought out the best in the former practicing medical doctor, Armand Hammer. In response to the emergency, Hammer recruited four American medical doctors, including two cancer specialists, and organized millions of dollars of medical supplies and assistance. Dr. Robert Gale, a bone marrow transplant specialist, was one those who assisted victims of the Chernobyl radiation. Gale and his colleagues, along with Russian doctors, performed more than 50 transplant operations in a few days, saving many lives. Gorbachev personally thanked the Americans, and Hammer personally, on Russian television.[41]

Averill Harriman

Harriman began his interest in Soviet – American trade with ocean trade – American ship and Commerce Corporation during the First World War. By 1920 he was involved with the Guarantee Trust

Corporation through his company, W.A. Harriman and Company, soon to invest in Derutra, the German-Soviet shipping line, the first joint venture in Soviet Russia.[42] By 1925, Harriman had invested in a new concession to exploit manganese in Russia. This was for the development of the Chiaturi deposits in Soviet Georgia. Both Harriman and the Soviets hoped this would lead to a strengthening of economic relations and further ties.[43]

Another important entrepreneur in the 1920s was Alexander Gumberg, who established the All-Russian Textile Syndicate in 1923. This syndicate focused on cotton purchases in the United States and quickly surpassed Alamerico in purchases by 1924. Gumberg, Russian born, was a strong advocate for better Russian–American relations, working with Raymond Robins in the revolutionary period. Gumberg always stressed the importance of commerce as key to improving Soviet–American relations.[44]

Other Concessionaires

The American engineer Washington Vanderlip launched the first effort for a concession in 1920, in Siberia. But this came to naught, as did the Sinclair Exploration Company's attempt at an oil concession in Siberia. Although both Vanderlip and Ludwig Martens believed, in the 1920s, that it was only a matter of time before things would be resolved. As Martens wrote to Vanderlip in 1921, "Your arrangements with the authorities in Moscow remain unaffected by these instructions and are a matter for action by those authorities."[45]

Trotsky, in a long interview in 1923, discussed American-Russian trade, and commented that he was "convinced that the American industrial and commercial world would recognize the importance of the Russian market" and Russia could "readily absorb increasing quantities of American products."

> There is also another important moral factor. . . which facilitates the closer union of Soviet Russia with the United States. In our papers and technical journals you will often meet the phrase "Americanism" and "Americanization" used in a favorable, not in a disparaging sense. The Russians are very eager to learn from the Americans the scientific organization of industry and of labor, and this forms a moral bond between Russia and America.[46]

Averill Harriman followed with a concession for manganese, from 1922 to 1926. The end of the New Economic Policy and the advent of Stalinist five-year plans brought an end to the concession policy.[47]

U.S. recognition of the USSR in 1933 also led to some interesting explorations of the possibility of cultural exchange. In 1937, the Soviets accepted an invitation by the United States to participate in an international exhibition in the United States in 1939 at the World's Fair, and also in 1937, Foreign Minister Litvinov accepted the congratulations of the United States for the flight of Soviet pilots over the North Pole to the United States. Litvinov hoped that the good feeling engendered might lead to new "cultural links" between the two countries.[48]

Finally, in 1937, the Soviets welcomed American naval ships to Vladivostok on a goodwill visit. Izvestia noted,

> the Soviet public sincerely welcomes the arrival in Vladivostok of the American guests under the leadership of Squadron Commander Admiral Yarnell. The most hearty and friendly reception will naturally be accorded to the guests. May this hearty and friendly reception be at least a partial answer to the hospitality and attention which were shown in the U.S.A. to the aviators of the Soviet Union and which will never be forgotten by our country.[49]

In 1938, another interesting link was forged between the two countries. For a number of years, every summer American Eskimos from the islands off Alaska visited relatives in the Chukotsk national region of Siberia. They came by boat in groups of 20 or 30. In 1938, through an exchange of notes the US and Soviet governments regularized these visits. The American Eskimos would be provided with certificates from the US government allowing their visit and the exchange of good seal and walrus skins for consumer goods in Russia. This arrangement lasted until 1948.[50]

Later in 1938, the USSR requested permission from the United States for two Soviet Navy research ships to visit Boston, San Francisco, and Alaska for purpose of taking on fuel, water, and supplies. This request was granted.[51]

Notes

1 Steffens to Fremont Older, October 5, 1923, in Eugene Anschel, ed., *American Appraisals of Soviet Russia, 1917–1977* (Metuchen, NJ: Scarecrow Press, 1978), 215.
2 Feuer, 120.
3 Ibid., 121.
4 Margaret Wettlin, *Fifty Russian Winters* (New York: John Wiley and Sons, 1994).
5 Wettlin, 49.
6 Ibid., 68.

7 Ibid., 113.
8 Ibid., 114.
9 Feuer, 122.
10 Ibid., 122.
11 Ibid., 126.
12 Muriel Lester, *It Occurred to Me* (New York: Harper and Brothers, 1937), 218.
13 Ibid., 218.
14 McMaster (AFSC Berlin) report on trip to Moscow, 1930, AFSC files.
15 Richenda Scott, *Quakers in Russia* (London: Michael Joseph, 1964), 272.
16 Scott, 276.
17 Ibid., 277.
18 Lawrence McK Miller, *Witness for Humanity: A Biography of Clarence Pickett* (Lancashire: Pendle Hill, 1999), 119.
19 Miller, 119.
20 Irwin Abrams, "The Moscow World Youth Forum of 1961: An American Friend's Experience of Quaker and Soviet Peacemaking," *Quaker History* 84, No. 2 (Fall, 1995): 144–145.
21 W.E.B. Dubois, *The Autobiography of W.E.B. Dubois* (New York: International Publishers, 1968/2007), 37.
22 Dubois, 43.
23 Katerina Clark, *Moscow the Fourth Rome* (Cambridge, MA: Harvard, 2011), 142.
24 Clark, 191.
25 David-Fox, 282–283.
26 See Michael Gelb, ed., *An American Engineer in Stalin's Russia, the Memoirs of Zara Witkin* (Berkely: University of California Press, 1991).
27 Gelb, 26.
28 Ibid., 26–27, 89, 105.
29 Joan Hoff Wilson, *Ideology and Economics: U.S. Relations with the Soviet Union, 1918–1933* (Columbia: University of Missouri Press, 1974).
30 Armand Hammer with Neil Lyndon, *Hammer* (New York: G.P. Putnam's Sons, 1987), 71.
31 Ibid., 87–88.
32 Katherine A.S. Siegel, *Loans and Legitimacy: The Evolution of Soviet-American Relations, 1919–1933* (Lexington: University of Kentucky Press, 1996), 78–79.
33 Siegel, 79.
34 Ibid., 80.
35 Ibid, 118.
36 Ibid., 80–81.
37 Hammer, 161–166.
38 Ibid., 322.
39 Ibid., 432–434.
40 Ibid., 400–430.
41 Ibid., 16–22.
42 Siegel, 123.
43 Moscow Economic Life, June 20, 1925 in Goldberg, Vol. 2, 260–261.
44 Ibid., 81–84.
45 Martens to Vanderlip, January 8, 1921 in Goldberg, Vol. 2, 222–223.

46 Trotsky interview, Soviet Russia, Vol. 8, September 1923, p. 270 in Goldberg, Vol. 2, 256.
47 Ibid., 122–126.
48 Harold J. Goldberg, ed., *Documents of Soviet-American Relations, Vol. 3, 1933–1941* (New York: Academic International Press, 1998), 177–178.
49 Izvestia July 29, 1937, in Goldberg, 182.
50 Exchange of notes, March 16 and April 28, 1938, in Goldberg, 202–203.
51 Troianoski to Hull, June 8, 1938, in Goldberg, 211.

6 1940s and 1950s

From the Grand Alliance to the Cultural Agreement

The 1940s continued in many ways the contacts and openings from the late 1920s and 1930s – business, religious groups, engineers, radicals, and fellow travelers – although the purges of the late 1930s put a damper on some initiatives. The Welles-Oumansky negotiations of 1940 between the United States and the USSR kept the door open, and Lend-Lease was extended to the USSR early in 1941. The Grand Alliance of 1941–1942 would seem to open up the possibility of even more exchanges and visits. But in truth, the major expansion was in culture. It could be said that the major thing tying together the United States and the Soviet Union during the Second World War was jazz. The exchanges of artists and musicians were breathtaking – Paul Robeson, Benny Goodman, Charlie Chaplin. Popular music transcended politics. The wartime alliance provided the single most important boost Soviet jazz had ever received.[1]

The jazz connection actually began much earlier. The young Leningrad pianist Leopold Teplitsky came to Philadelphia in 1926 determined to master the techniques of American jazz, to purchase arrangements and musical instruments, and start a new jazz orchestra for Leningrad. Interestingly, Teplitsky's trip was sponsored by none other than Lenin's Commissar of Public Enlightenment, Anatoly Lunacharsky.[2]

By 1934, the connections began to mature. The editors of the journal *Soviet Music* declared to their readers, "the goal of our journal is to strengthen the ties between the USSR and the USA in musical performance, study and criticism."[3]

As Starr recounts,

> the most important monument to this official interest was a series of lectures on the history of dance music, delivered in Leningrad by the respected musicologist and critic Mikhail Druskin in the winter of 1935. Druskin highlighted the importance of jazz.[4]

DOI: 10.4324/9781003190967-7

As Andrei Gromyko, the long-time Soviet Foreign Minister remarked on the great influence of American jazz on the Soviet Union of the 1940s and early 1950s. Paul Robeson was the key figure. He visited many times and was always greeted warmly. As Gromyko remembered,

> we used to have impassioned conversations. I once read him some verses of Pushkin and he asked me to write them out for him. We Soviet people will remember him as a friend and supporter of good relations between our two states. He loved both countries, if in different ways.[5]

The importance of jazz in the cultural contacts of the 1940s and 1950s cannot be overstated. Many in the Eisenhower administration began to see that American jazz just might be America's edge in the Cold War. In his State of the Union Address in 1953, Ike discussed the Cold War as a struggle for world public opinion. Both the USIA and Voice of America were created. But a major problem in public opinion was the existence of segregation. Jazz was one way to deal with it. Adam Clayton Powell, African American Congressman from New York, urged Ike to send "jazz ambassadors" to Russia and eastern Europe to deal forthrightly both with culture and with political issues. So, in the mid-1950s, Dizzy Gillespie went to Russia. He dealt openly with political issues and did not apologize. On Voice of America, Music USA was begun and proved very popular, especially with jazz artists. In 1956, Louis Armstrong made a tour of the USSR, followed by Duke Ellington and Dave Brubeck.

As Margaret Wettlin found in the midst of the war in 1943, American music remained wildly popular in Russia. To honor American Independence Day, the Moscow Conservatory staged a concert of American music. The Moscow State Symphony opened with "When Johnny Comes Marching Home," and stars of the Bolshoi Theatre sang American songs, including "My Old Kentucky Home." The concert ended with a rendition of Gershwin's "Rhapsody in Blue."[6]

Nor was African-American music in Russia limited to jazz. The Blues were also wildly popular. American visitor and chronicler Andrea Lee relates the tour of B.B. King in Russia in 1978. King toured the Soviet Union for three weeks, introducing a wide range of Russians to something they had never heard: the Blues. As Lee related,

> B.B. King is a great warm presence when he performs, and he asks his audience to pour themselves out to him in return . . . An older man. looked thoughtful as we talked to him. . . B.B. King

astounded me. This blues music – it's not like jazz. He poured his whole heart and soul out there on the stage. Such feeling is very Russian – we believe in emotion, in the soul. I never thought that an American could feel that way."[7]

When JFK succeeded Ike as President he expanded these tours, believing that the jazz ambassadors provided a cultural bridge. Benny Goodman and Duke Ellington took an eight city tour. While Kennedy's assassination ended this tour, the United States had learned that through jazz, we could listen to the world and engage with issues of race.[8]

One very important visit to the USSR was taken in 1943 by Wendell Willkie. As he remarked, "We have got to understand each other," I said.

> We have got to learn to know each other. We are allies in this war, and the American people will not let you down until Hitler has been defeated. But I would like to see us work together in the peace as well as after it. This will require great patience and great tolerance and great understanding on both sides.[9]

The author W.L. White took a six-week trip to the USSR in 1944 and had many exchanges with local Russians. Most striking perhaps was his portrayal of a toast he gave at a banquet in Moscow:

> I am most happy to be here to meet the writers, sculptors, and musicians of the Soviet Union. It is a most happy occasion that we can meet with the creative people of the country. In the future I look forward to closer bonds between soviet cultural leaders and those of America.[10]

The American Friends Service Committee had won the Nobel Peace Prize in 1947 for its relief work in the aftermath of the Second World War. AFSC Executive Secretary Clarence Pickett was determined to use the prize and the publicity it engendered to explore better relations between the United States and the Soviet Union. This first resulted in a report, *the United States and the Soviet Union: Some Quaker Proposals for Peace* (Yale University Press, 1949).

> In the light of Quaker experience in dealing with human beings of many different nationalities and in many different parts of the world we believe that an extension of opportunities for personal

relations between Russians and Americans could be a benefit to both peoples.[11]

The first concrete expression of this hope was a visit of Quakers from London Yearly Meeting to the Soviet Union in 1951. A highlight was Leslie Metcalf's testimony to the Moscow Baptist Church: "The Society of Friends to which we all belong attached the greatest importance to direct and personal contact between peoples and we rejoice in this opportunity to come into personal relationship with you and your fellow countrymen."[12]

In a meeting with the Minister of Education, they discussed future exchanges, which the minister supported. Following this visit, American Friends, encouraged by AFSC, planned their own visit, which took place in 1955.

The AFSC pioneered in exchanges of scientists, physicians, and scholars and brought business leaders in off-the-record meetings with soviet leaders to promote trade. Moreover, they organized yearly seminars and conferences with U.S. and soviet leaders.[13] As Feffer and AFSC argue, "government proposals are not sufficient. Internationalism should also entail the joining together of citizens from various countries. . . . activists, East and West, could cooperate on a program targeting both NATO and the Warsaw Pact."[14]

Other American religious groups also pursued opportunities for personal connections with Russian church leaders and parishioners. The Methodist leader Ralph Sockman made the case for such connections in a 1954 piece, "To see behind curtains":

> If we are to have mutual understanding between nations, we must see the human situations behind the published news, the faces behind the facts. . . I can still hear the Russian Baptists praying for their fellow churchmen in America.[15]

The 1950s saw direct and institutional connections finally established between American Protestant churches and the Russian Orthodox Church and the Evangelical and Christian Baptists. A small delegation of American church leaders, headed by Eugene Carson Blake, the President of the National Council of Churches, set out on a mission to contact co-believers in the Soviet Union and to establish relations with sister churches. A series of exchanges followed, and by 1961 the Protestant and Orthodox Churches of the Soviet Union became members of the World Council of Churches.[16]

Another aspect of the multi-phasic efforts of the USIA to change the perception of the world toward the United States was the "peoples' capitalism" campaign of the 1950s. "Peoples capitalism" was meant to be a positive effort, pursued through radio and print, and all U.S. embassies abroad, to portray U.S. capitalism as benefitting the great majority of people in the United States – good jobs, material prosperity, rising standard of living, health care, education, Social Security, and dealing with social problems.[17]

A key element in this enhanced propaganda and information campaign was the exploitation of trade fairs and exhibits. Over 20 exhibitions were mounted in the 1950s, including Bangkok, Brussels, Paris, Zagreb, and New Delhi. A new feature of several of the exhibits was a pavilion on "unfinished work," focused on racial discrimination, urban renewal, and conservation. Each exhibit had three sections: one focused on the problem, one on what was being done to address it, and the last focused on the future.[18]

But the biggest effort was made for the 1958–1959 Exhibition in Moscow, in Sokolniki Park, where U.S. and Soviet pavilions competed side by side. The American exhibition was massive, with major contributions from U.S. corporations. Exhibits included computers, food, furnishings, culture, and of course the famous "model kitchen" of the Nixon-Khrushchev exchange. A major new factor of the U.S. exhibition was the presence of 75 young American, Russian-speaking guides, which were one of the hits of the exhibition.[19] A particular highpoint, usually mobbed by Russians, was the Pepsi-Cola exhibit. Even Khrushchev loved it. This led to Pepsi being introduced in the Soviet Union, where it soon became a favorite beverage.[20]

The path to the breakthrough U.S.–Soviet cultural and educational exchange agreement of 1958 was long and arduous, beginning with a Soviet proposal of 1953 and continuing through Quaker missions of 1955 and numerous cultural exchanges of the mid-1950s. The subject was discussed repeatedly at top-level meetings of soviet and American negotiators in Geneva in 1955, finally resulting in the agreement of 1957–1958.

As Khrushchev notes in his memoirs about his exchanges with Dulles:

> Dulles often said that the goal of the United States was to push socialism in Europe back to the borders of the Soviet Union, and he seemed to be obsessed with the idea of encirclement. He extended America's economic embargo of the Soviet Union to include a boycott on cultural exchange. Not even Soviet tourists and chess players were permitted to visit the United States.[21]

The immediate origins of the 1957–1958 cultural agreement between the United States and the Soviet Union can be found as far back as 1953 (not counting all of the earlier antecedents detailed above). Soon after the death of Stalin in 1953, the Soviet Union as part of Khrushchev's "peaceful coexistence" campaign eased restrictions on travel. Over 100 U. S. private citizens were admitted to the USSR in 1953. This new policy was strongly supported by Soviet intellectuals such as Ilya Ehrenburg and Dmitri Shostakovich.[22] The U.S. policy in 1953 was still restrictive, due to the perception of the "communist threat" and so, according to the National security council report of March, 1955, the United States was

> placed in a paradoxical position. . . Despite its traditional policy favoring freedom of travel and its record of having favored a liberal exchange of persons with the USSR in the postwar period, the U.S. is accused of maintaining "an iron curtain" and these accusations are being made not only by representatives of international communism but also by otherwise friendly persons in the free world. The situation is causing damage and may cause further damage to US prestige and the US reputation for liberal world leadership.[23]
>
> US admission of a larger but still modest number of European Soviet bloc nationals . . . would tend to maintain the reputation of the U.S. as a mature leader and a believer in freedom. Such admission would thus counter communist propaganda and tend to strengthen free world cooperation with the U.S.[24]
>
> . . . on balance,. . . the advantages to the US of a broadened admission policy outweigh the disadvantages. Such disadvantages will be more than counterbalanced by upholding the US reputation for adherence to the principles of cultural exchange and freedom of movement. . ..[25]

The NSC also broadened the admission into the United States by mail of communist and Soviet periodicals.[26]

Others, like NY Times Moscow correspondent Harrison Salisbury, supported the expansion of cultural contacts, believing that the change in atmosphere in the Soviet Union following the death of Stalin was a propitious time to pursue such a strategy. Salisbury had no doubt that expanded exchange would rebound to the benefit of the United States.[27]

An interesting breakthrough came in the summer of 1955 when an Iowa newspaper, responding to Khrushchev's call for increased corn production, invited a Soviet delegation to come to Iowa. To everyone's amazement, the invitation was accepted.[28]

As Hixson relates, by the time of the second foreign ministers conference in the fall of 1955, a consensus had begun to emerge in Washington concerning a new strategy for waging the Cold War emphasizing cultural interaction, penetration, and exchange. Eisenhower was strongly supportive, and the director of the U.S. Information Agency, Theodore Streibert, pursued it vigorously, advocating "a bold dramatic step to substantially increase what we are doing in the whole area of information exchange and contacts – the exchange of ideas and people."[29]

The Directive to Foreign Ministers in Geneva, July 23, 1955, noted

> the foreign Ministers should by means of experts study measures, including those possible in organs and agencies of the United Nations, which could (a) bring about a progressive elimination of barriers which interfere with free communications and peaceful trade between people and (b) bring about such freer contacts and exchanges as are to the mutual advantage of the countries and peoples concerned.[30]

During the July meetings in Geneva (British, French, the United States, Soviet), there was extensive discussion of east–west contacts. Eisenhower reported on these meetings on July 25, noting that

> the subject that took most of our attention in this regard was the possibility of increased visits by citizens of one country into the territory of another, doing this in such a way as to give each the fullest possible opportunity to learn about the people of the other nation. In this particular subject there was the greatest possible degree of agreement. As a matter of fact, this agreement often repeated and enthusiastically supported by the words of the members of each side.[31]

Evidence of this can be found in the record of the President's dinner, from July 18, 1955:

> Premier Bulganin. . . mentioned that the Soviet government entirely supported the suggestion that there should be greater contact between our people. In this connection, mention was made that the agriculturists from both countries had arrived in the United States and the USSR yesterday. The President observed that these delegations were small and said there should have been 200. Premier

Bulganin said he quite agreed that he would be prepared to increase such exchanges. The President pointed out that he would do his best to facilitate such exchanges but the development of the appropriate atmosphere would take time and he could not say what Congress would do in the connection but that the Premier could count on his support for developing these exchanges.[32]

Eisenhower in a telegram to the Department of State of July 23, let it be known in no uncertain terms what he believed:

Gentlemen, the agenda item for today's discussion is the development of contacts between east and west. Now, accordingly today we might discuss methods of normalizing and increasing the contest between our nations in many fields. I am heartened by the deep interest in this question which interest implies a common purpose to understand each other. . . To help achieve the goal of peace based on justice and right and mutual understanding, there are certain concrete steps that could be taken: first, to lower the barriers which now impeded the interchange of information and ideas between our peoples; Two, to lower the barriers which impeded the opportunities of people to travel anywhere in the world for peaceful, friendly purposes so that we all will have a chance to know each other face to face.[33]

In the aftermath of Geneva, both sides talked repeatedly about expanding cultural contacts and exchanges, although no definitive agreements were reached. Eisenhower reported in a radio/television speech that increased contacts had been the point of greatest agreement between the two sides in Geneva, although he was contradicted by Secretary of State Dulles.[34]

Despite Eisenhower and Streibert's support, Dulles continued to oppose expanding cultural contacts, and the Foreign Ministers meeting of October, 1955, was unable to resolve the impasse. Instead, groups and individuals took advantage of the greater openness on both sides. Major Soviet musicians such as David Oistrakh and Mstislav Rostropovich toured the United States in the fall and winter of 1955–1956, and more than 2,000 American scholars, artists, religious leaders, educators, and writers visited the USSR during this same period.[35]

A major contributor to the developing spirit of exchange was the original transnational anti-nuclear movement – the Pugwash conference on Science and world Affairs, which first convened in 1955 (building on a statement drafted by Bertrand Russell and Albert Einstein) and would bring together scientists from both countries on a regular basis well into the 1990s. Pugwash would win the Nobel Peace Prize in 1995.[36]

Another scientists' movement, the International Physicians for the Prevention of Nuclear War (IPPNW), worked with physicians in both countries to call attention to the danger of nuclear war and to press for test ban, arms reductions, and negotiations. Key to the organization were Soviet physician Dr. Yevgeniy Chazov and U.S. counterpart Dr. Bernard Lown.[37]

Similarly important were the series of conferences initiated by Norman Cousins at the suggestion of President Eisenhower, of scientists and policy makers called the Dartmouth Conferences, held at Dartmouth College on a regular basis from 1960 to 1991.[38]

By the Khrushchev era in the 1950s, bilateral scientists meetings had become de rigueur. Khrushchev by 1959 had come to the conclusion that these meetings were an important way to build international pressure for disarmament. His relationship with the physicist Leo Szilard was important in this regard. Szilard and Khrushchev spent many hours together developing and furthering this idea, which would lead to a whole series of bilateral scientific meetings, in part funded by the Ford Foundation.[39]

These meetings were so important and long-lasting, having major impact on U.S. and Soviet policy, that they have been called an embryonic transnational civil society.[40] They were perhaps most successful in influencing soviet leaders than they were with Americans, and they reached their zenith under Gorbachev and his foreign minister Eduard Shevardnadze.[41]

On the citizen level, a key transnational activist movement was the Nevada-Semipalatinsk movement, which protested nuclear testing both in Nevada and in Kazakhstan. The protests in Kazakhstan was the largest in Soviet history.[42] The massive number of protestors eventually shut down the main Soviet nuclear test range and helped persuade the Soviet Union, the United States, Britain, and France to halt testing.[43]

Perhaps the most successful means of changing the cultural understanding of the United States in the Soviet Union was radio, and particularly music on the radio. The Voice of America, while continuing its commentaries, feature programs, and news, began to see that music, and particularly jazz, was essential to building new audiences. The wildly popular "Music USA," begun in 1955, may have done more to change the image of the United States in the Soviet Union than anything else.[44]

Following closely on the heels of Music USA was the agreement reached for exchange of slick magazines – *Amerika*, and USSR. Amerika was extremely popular in the Soviet Union and featured articles reprinted from popular American magazines like *Colliers, Life, Look, Reader's Digest,* and *The Saturday Evening Post.* Emphasis was on daily life in America, and positive articles on race relations were often featured.[45]

Scholarly exchanges began in 1956, building on a proposal of Professor Martin Malia of the University of California, Berkeley, for both graduate students and faculty scholars. Robert Cutler of the NSC noted that "the U.S. has much more to gain from such an exchange than the USSR."[46]

Ike was strongly in favor of all the cultural exchange ideas, and many others noted that this change in U.S. policy was made at Geneva in accordance with the President's own decision. The new policy was that the "United states should take the initiative in East-West exchanges as a positive instrument of U.S. foreign policy."[47]

Dulles finally rethought his opposition to this policy and endorsed the new National Security Council policy paper, NSC 5607 (June 29, 1956), which advocated a multiphasic program of cultural exchange and information and became the basis for U.S. policy until the signing of the cultural exchange agreement of 1958.[48]

In accordance with this new policy, the United States invited Soviets (and east European states) to send observers for the Presidential Election of 1956, which they accepted.

The United States suspended exchanges in late 1956, as a consequence of the soviet invasion of Hungary, but renewed them in February 1957.[49]

A great advocate for citizen exchange in the Eisenhower administration was Nelson Rockefeller. Rockefeller was one of the first to propose a multiphasic exchange of students, teachers, scientists, business leaders, artists, dancers, singer, and any group that would help us reach out to the communists especially in the USSR.[50]

> The first US-Soviet exchange agreement, signed on January 27, 1958, represented an attempt to initiate a dialogue between two states separated by political ideology and distance. . . Once regarded as only a footnote to political relations between the two countries, exchanges today are recognized as a vital element in the efforts by the two superpowers to achieve a more stable relationship.[51]

Ike continued to pursue initiatives on cultural exchange. In February 1958, he proposed asking some 10,000 Russian students to come to the United States, at the expense of the U.S. government, to spend a year in American colleges. The idea was not altogether a propaganda stunt – Eisenhower was a great believer in promoting international understanding through exchange of students. In a handwritten draft of a letter to Bulganin proposing the idea, he declared, "For if history teaches us anything, it is this: Nothing but evil has ever come of misunderstanding. And nothing but good has ever come of genuine increased understanding between fellow human beings."[52]

Another notable citizen intervention was that of journalist and activist Norman Cousins, on behalf of the partial nuclear test ban between the United States and the Soviet Union.

> Between 1958 and 1962, as the Geneva talks dragged on, both Sane and Cousins worked to mobilize public opinion behind the need for the treaty as a first step toward defusing East-West tensions. Cousins was particularly influential in this process, even acting as an unofficial liaison between President Kennedy and Soviet Premier Khrushchev in helping break an impasse in the negotiations. . . in late April, 1963, Cousins conferred with Khrushchev at his Black Sea retreat for over seven hours. Cousins told the premier how a number of citizens organizations had come together in the United States to develop public support for the President's position in favor of a test ban treaty, and how Kennedy encouraged the campaign from its inception. . . After reviewing several problems in soviet American relations, Khrushchev finally acknowledged his belief in Kennedy's sincere interest in a test ban treaty, and agreed to join the United States in making a fresh start in negotiations.[53]

The signing of the Cultural Exchange Agreement of 1958 unleashed a wide range of exchanges, from students to professors to artists, agriculturalists, businessmen and many other professions. The proliferation of such programs continued through the late 1950s, 1960s, and 1970s and prepared the way for the new surge of citizen diplomacy that characterized the end of the Cold War in the 1980s.

One of the important breakthrough results of cultural exchange agreement was breaking the impasse in U.S.–Soviet film exchange. Within months of the signing of the cultural agreement U.S. films such as *Mr. Smith Goes to Washington*, the Tarzan films, *Roman Holiday*, *The Old Man and the Sea*, and *Oklahoma*. In return. Soviet films such as *The Idiot*, *Don Quixote*, *War and Peace,* and *Swan Lake* traveled to the United States.[54]

But even more successful than American films in Russia were American artists. The biggest hit of all was van Cliburn in the Tchaikovsky International Music Competition in Moscow in April, 1958. Van Cliburn won the competition, wowing Soviet audiences and doing much to disabuse all who saw him or heard about him that the United States was "culturally backward."[55]

Despite Eisenhower's emphasis on student exchange, far short of his hoped for 10,000 students traveled from the USSR to the United States in the first years following the agreement. This gradually increased and was given a boost by the Moscow world /festival of Youth, which brought more than 30,000 young people from around the world to Moscow. As Walter Hixson has argued, "the Moscow youth festival marked a turning point in Soviet cultural history. . . t/he /soviet public received unprecedented exposure to western youth, music, fashion, consumer goods, ideas, and political perspectives. The festival left a permanent cultural imprint."[56]

Notes

1 Starr, 191.
2 Frederick Starr, *Red and Hot*, 66.
3 Starr, 160.
4 Ibid.
5 Andrei Gromyko, *Memoirs* (New York: Doubleday, 1989), 62–63.
6 Wettlin, 240.
7 Andrea Lee, *Russian Journal* (New York: Random House, 1979), 172, 175.
8 PBS documentary, "The Jazz Ambassadors", February 2, 2021. See also *Red and Hot*.
9 Wendell Wilkie, *One World* (New York: Simon and Schuster, 1943), 98–99.
10 W.L. White, *Report on the Russians* (New York: Harcourt, Brace, and Co., 1945), 162–163.
11 *The US and the Soviet Union: Some Quaker Proposals for Peace* (London: Yale, 1949), 9.
12 Leslie Metcalf, Excerpts from notes on the Quaker Mission to Moscow, October 4, 1951, AFSC files.
13 John Feffer, *Beyond Détente: Soviet Foreign Policy and U.S. Options* (New York: Noonday Press (farrar, Strauss and Giroux), 1990), ix.
14 Feffer, 159.
15 Ralph Sockman, "The Meaning of Peace," in *Plowshares and Pruning Hooks* (Chicago, IL: IVP Academic, 1954), 24–25.
16 Bruce Rigdon, "Religious Faith in Soviet American Relations," in Daniel N. Nelson and Roger B. Anderson, *Soviet American Relations: Understanding Differences, Avoiding Conflict* (Wilmington, DE: Scholarly Resources, 1988), 61–62.
17 Hixson, 132–134.
18 Ibid., 144–146.
19 Ibid., 171.
20 Ibid., 169.

21 Nikita Khrushchev, *Khrushchev Remembers* (New York: Little Brown, 1970), 398.
22 Walter Hixson, *Parting the Curtain: Propaganda, Culture and the Cold War* (New York: St. Martins, 1998), 102
23 NSC 550811, March 26, 1955, FRUS 1955–1957, Vol. XXIV, 200–201.
24 Ibid., 202.
25 Ibid., 203.
26 Ibid., 206.
27 Hixson, 103.
28 Ibid., 104.
29 Theodore Streibert, Memorandum for the President, September 4, 1955, General Correspondence and Memoranda series, Box 3, John Foster Dulles Papers, Eisenhower Library, as quoted in Hixson, 104.
30 Department of State Bulletin 33, No. 840 (August 1, 1955), 177. See also Gordon Weihmiler, *U.S.-Soviet Summits, an Account of East West Diplomacy at the Top, 1955–1985* (Georgetown University, Institute for the Study of Diplomacy, 1990).
31 Ibid., 210–211.
32 Memorandum for the Record, July 18, 1955, FRUS 1955–1957, Vol. 374.
33 FRUS 1955–1957, Vol. V, 475–476.
34 Walter L. Hixson, *Parting the Curtain: Propaganda, Culture and the Cold War* (New York: St. Martin's Griffin Press, 1998), 101.
35 Hixson, 107.
36 Matthew Evangelista, *Unarmedd Forces: The Transnational Movement to End the Cold War* (Ithaca, NY: Cornell University Press, 1999), 3.
37 Evangelista, 5.
38 Ibid., 32.
39 Ibid., 36–37.
40 Ibid., 39.
41 Ibid., 184–185.
42 Ibid., 9.
43 Ibid., 351–356.
44 Hixson, 115.
45 Ibid., 118–119.
46 Robert Cutler to the Secretary of State, February 10, 1956, Hixson, 218–219.
47 Ibid., 241–242.
48 Hixson, 108–109.
49 Ibid., 254–256.
50 Harold Stassen and Marshall Houts, *Eisenhower Turning the World Toward Peace* (St. Paul, MN: Merrill-Magnus Publishing, 1991), 350.
51 US-Soviet Exchange: The Next Thirty Years Conference Report, Eisenhower World Affairs Institute, 1988.
52 Draft letter, Eisenhower to Bulganin, February 24, 1958, Ann Whitman Series, Eisenhower Library, quoted in Stephen F. Ambrose, *Eisenhower the President*, Vol. II (New York: Simon and Shuster, 1984), 445.
53 "Norman Cousins" in DeBenedetti, 184–185.
54 Hixson, 154–155.
55 Ibid., 156.
56 Ibid., 159.

7 Looking Forward

The range of cultural and citizen exchange activities of the 1980s are multifaceted and notable. I will only hint at some of them here, but it is important to note that none of them would have been possible without the strong basis laid by the agreements of 1955–1958. As the Eisenhower World Affairs Institute noted in its summary, "Thirty Years of U.S.–Soviet Exchange," quoting Charles Wick, the Director of the US Information Agency,

> The complexity of both American and Soviet societies demands that contacts be established not only between states but between peoples. It is not enough to leave the relationship in the hands of officials of both sides. To do so is to risk a relationship that is brittle and vulnerable to the vagaries of U.S.-Soviet political relations. In a nuclear age, we cannot afford to do this.[1]

At the conference in Gettysburg Pennsylvania, the participants, both Soviet and American, reiterated their commitment to carry on and expand exchanges, and focused on some key factors necessary for such expansion: how exchange affects the political bilateral relationship and vice versa the impact of technological advancements on exchanges, problems of and differences in communication and administration; how the differing roles of private and public sector participants affect coordination; the role of exchange during times of political crisis problems associated with reciprocity in exchange; and the critical problem of funding stability and availability.[2]

The International Conference for Disarmament and Détente, 2nd Vienna Dialogue in November 1983, worked mostly on proposals for disarmament, but the special interest group on Cultural Workers stressed the importance of international exchanges with artists and cultural workers, "to advance the good will necessary to ensure the

DOI: 10.4324/9781003190967-8

peaceful existence of all countries. Particular emphasis was placed on the importance of cultural exchanges with the soviet Union and all other socialist countries to promote a better international understanding."[3]

The 1980s were full of exchanges, and the transnational connections forged were essential to the end of the Cold War, as Mathew Evangelists has argued extensively in his study, Unarmed Forces: the transnational movement to end the Cold War.[4]

One of the first pioneers in this work was Sharon Tennison, who took her first trip with others to the Soviet Union in 1983. Tennison continued visits and exchanges well into the twenty-first century, redoubling her efforts after the Russian intervention in Ukraine in 2014. Tennison established the Center for Citizen Initiatives to promote these exchanges. This became the model for people-to people diplomacy, with Americans traveling to Russia, and Russians to America. Her work was often questioned by the FBI, the KGB, and ordinary citizens who sometimes suspected she was a foreign agent. But always after questioning, she was able to resume her work. One interesting unexpected result of her work occurred in 1985 when she was asked in Leningrad whether there were any effective treatments for alcoholism in the United States. This resulted in the first Alcoholics Anonymous chapter in the Soviet Union, which has continued to grow ever since. She has made strong personal links with Mikhail Gorbachev and other Soviet leaders.[5] But what has most affected Tennison over the years has been her interaction with individual Soviet and Russian citizens. As she relates, "they were friendly, curious, eager to know more about America and Americans. And they were terribly concerned about peace, terribly afraid of nuclear war."[6]

As Don Carlson and Craig Comstock argue in their study Citizen Summitry,

> thousands of citizens have begun a new kind of diplomacy – taking care not to speak for their government, but showing openness, persistence, and flair in representing much that's best and most creative about America. These citizen diplomats enlarge the opportunities for productive relations between peoples and, by extension, between their governments.[7]
>
> The way to normalize relations between the two cultures is not to send old men to Geneva or any other part of the world to sign pieces of paper claiming that they will trust each other into the future. The only way to normalize relations is for Americans and Russians to develop normal relation with each other.[8]

More than 50,000 Americans are now visiting Russia every year. Although not all of them consider themselves "citizen diplomats," they are having a wide array of contacts, with Russians of every stripe.[9]

As Edward Everett Hale wrote centuries ago, "I am only one But still I am one. I cannot do everything, But still I can do something; And because I cannot do everything, I will not refuse to do the Something that I can do."[10]

> Most of the new diplomats believe in the importance of long-term relationships. If Americans and Soviets simply have short diplomatic encounters, they may be able to exchange information and improve their mutual understand, but they will never truly appreciate – let alone be capable of permanently tolerating and co-operating with – one another's differences. This is why the new diplomats are increasingly committed to spending many years, even decades, nurturing their ties with soviets.[11]

President Ronald Reagan expounded upon all the different ways that citizen contacts could strengthen Russian-American ties:

> We could look to increase scholarship programs; improve language studies; conduct course in history, culture, and other subjects; develop new sister-cities; establish libraries and cultural centers; and yes, increase athletic competition People of both our nations love sports. If we must compete, let it be on the playing fields and not the battlefield.
>
> In science and technology, we could launch new joint space ventures, and establish joint medical-research projects. In communications, we'd like to see more appearances in the other's mass media by representatives of both our countries .... people to people contacts can build genuine constituencies for peace in both countries.
>
> Such exchanges can build in our societies thousands of coalitions for cooperation and peace, . . . 'governments can only do so much; once they get the ball rolling, they should step out of the way and let people get together to share, enjoy, help, listen, and learn from each other . . . .
>
> It is not an impossible dream that our children and grandchildren can someday travel freely back and for the between America and the 'Soviet Union; visit each other's homes; work and study together; enjoy and discuss plays, music, and television, and root for teams when they compete.[12]

The American citizen-diplomats were not the only ones. There were also numerous Soviet counterparts working hard on their side. Their work is neatly encapsulated by a verse from the poetic volume, *Fuku* by Yevgeny Yevtushenko:

"In every border post
     There's something insecure.
Each one of them
     Is longing for leaves and flowers . . .
I suppose
     That at first, it was people who invented borders
And then borders
     Started to invent people . . . ;
Thank God,
     We have invisible thread and threadlets
Born of the threads of blood
          From the nails in the palms of Christ
These threads struggle through
          Tearing apart the barbed wire,
Leading love to join love . . . .
While borders still stand
          We are all in prehistory.
Real history will start
          When all borders are gone . . .
From all those thousands of borders
          'we have lost the only human one –
The borer between good and evil.
But while we still have invisible threads
Joining each self
          \with millions of selves.
There are no real superpower states.
Any fragile soul on this earth
          Is the real superpower.
My government is the whole family of man, all at once . . .
I am a racist,
I recognize only one race –
The race of all races.
How foreign is the word foreigner!
I have four and a half billion leaders
And I dance my Russian,
          My death-defying dance
On the invisible threads
That connect the hearts of people."[13]

Gale Warner has written an account of a number of these intrepid Soviet citizens in the 1980s –

> individuals who were unobtrusively moving forward projects that might bring the countries closer together. These Soviets were translating and distributing anti-nuclear books, matching children with American pen pals, inviting westerners into their homes, and coordinating exchanges. They were building lively personal networks across previously silent borders . . ."[14]

These individuals did not like to be called "peace activists" or even "citizen-diplomats." They preferred the Russian word "mirotvortsi" or "peace creators."[15] A good example is Olga Bazanova, of the Association of Siberian Families for Interrelationship and mutual understanding between the peoples of the USSR and the US. Olga believes that "the secret to peace lies in shared laughter over home-cooked meals and high-spirited parties full of dance and song."[16]

Another key individual is Ekaterina Podoltsova of the Group to Establish Trust, founded in 1982. This group called for the creation of a four-part dialogue between government leaders and citizens on both sides and sponsored demonstrations and seminars. Many of their members were arrested and charged with anti-Soviet behavior. They initiated more direct action beginning in 1984, including planting a peace garden in front of a Moscow police station and holding signs saying "flowers not bombs."[17]

Andrei Orlov is one of the activists who takes seriously the necessity of acting personally to change things. He objects to the term "citizen-diplomat" because he says he is neither. "Citizen means nationalism, means borders and separate nations. And diplomat means states, means governments. What we are doing is contrary to both of those things."[18]

Even the official Soviet Peace Committee has individuals that can be called citizen diplomats. Under the leadership of the new President Genrikh Borovik and others like Tair Tairov and Anatoly Belyaev, the editor of their journal, *XX Century and Peace*, the Soviet Peace Committee began to act more like their American counterparts. Frank discussions ensued, and a new group, the Foundation for Social Innovation, was spawned by their members.[19]

Yet another group having an impact in the Perestroika-Soviet Union of the late 1980s was that led by Galina Dolya. They focused on children, and pen-pal exchanges with children in the United States. These pen-pals eventually organized a fifth grade trip of Russian children to the United States, sponsored by Educators for Social Responsibility.[20]

All of this is best summed up by a poem by Bulat Okudshava:

"I'll bury a grape seed in the warm earth
I'll kiss the vine, I'll gather the ripe bunches
I'll call my friends together
And I'll tune my heart to love –
What else is there to live for
On this eternal earth?"[21]

Notes

1 "Thirty Years of U.S.-Soviet Exchange: A Project Overview," Eisenhower World Affairs Institute, 1988.
2 Ibid.
3 Documents, 2nd Vienna Dialogue: International Conference for Disarmament and Détente, November 14–127, 1983, Helsinki, 32.
4 Matthew Evangelista, *Unarmed Forces: The Transnational Movement to End the Cold War* (Ithaca, NY: Cornell University Press, 1999). See also David S. Meyer, "Political Opportunity after the Cold War," *Peace & Change* 19, No. 2 (April, 1994): 114–140.
5 Fred Weir, "How One Woman's Citizen Diplomacy Has Strengthened US-Russia Ties for Decades," *Christian Science Monitor*, December 17, 2018.
6 Don Carlson and Craig Comstock, ed., *Citizen Summitry* (Los Angeles, CA: Jeremy Tarcher, 1986), 107.
7 Carlson and Comstock, 60.
8 Ibid., 85–86.
9 Ibid., 99.
10 Quoted in Ibid., 97.
11 Ibid., 129.
12 Ibid., 134.
13 Yevgeny Yevtushenko, "Fuku," (1987) in Gale Warner, *The Invisible Threads: Independent Soviets Working for Global Awareness and Social Transformation* (Washington, DC: Seven Locks Press, 1991), frontspiece.
14 Warner, 1.
15 Ibid., 2.
16 Ibid., 53.
17 Ibid., 79–81.
18 Ibid., 98.
19 Warner, 112–149, 189–215. I can personally attest to this new spirit, being sponsored by the Foundation for Social Innovation on a trip to the USSR in 1982.
20 Warner, 155.
21 Ibid., 242.

Conclusion

Any focus on the 1980s as the center of U.S.–Soviet citizen diplomacy must ignore the incredible work done in the revolutionary period, the 1920s, 1930s, 1940s, and 1950s. It is not too strong to say that without the pathbreaking work by American activists, church leaders, Quakers, social workers, entrepreneurs, and artists, there would have been no breakthroughs in 1957–1958 and no brilliant successes of the 1980s. In particular, I would highlight the study seminars of Sherwood Eddy in the 1920s, and the jazz artists of the 1940s for establishing the groundwork which made the cultural and educational exchanges of later years possible.

Bibliography

A. Archival Collections

Action Chretienne des Etudiants Russe (Russian Student Christian Movement Archive, Paris).

Archives of the American Friends Service Committee and the Fellowship of Reconciliation, Swarthmore Peacer Collection, Swarthmore College.

Archives of the Friends War Victims Relief Committee and the Friends Service Council, Friends House, London.

Bakhmeteff Archives, Columbia University, New York City.

Emma Goldman Papers, Bancroft Library, University of California, Berkeley.

GARF (Gosudarstvennyi Arkhiv Rossiiskoi Federatsii (State Archive of the Russian Federation), Moscow. Reports from the Ministry of Internal Affairs and the State Economic Archive Concerning the Activities of the Russian Student Christian Movement and Foreign Aid Workers during the Great Famine.

Harry Emerson Fosdick Papers, Union Theological Seminary, New York.

Jane Addams Papers, Swarthmore Peace Collection, Swarthmore College.

John D. Rockefeller Papers, Rockefeller Archives, Tarrytown, NY.

John LaFarge, S.J. Papers, Jesuit Province of New York.

John Reed Papers, Harvard University.

Kautz Family YMCA Archives, University of Minnesota Libraries, Minneapolis.

L'Institut de Theologie Orthodoxe Saint-Serge (St. Sergius Orthodox Theological Institute Archive, Paris).

Paul B Anderson Papers, University of Illinois at Urbana-Champaign Archives.

Sherwood Eddy and Kirby Page Papers, Claremont School of Theology, Claremont, California.

Various Quaker family collections, Quaker Collection, Haverford College.

Various unpublished and undigitized papers at the Herbert Hoover Presidential Library, West Branch, Iowa, and the Hoover Institute on War, Revolution and Peace, Stanford University.

William and Glenora McFadden Papers, Duke University Archives.

World Student Christian Federation Archives, Yale Divinity School.

B. Printed Primary and Secondary Sources

Addison, Barbara. *Pragmatic Pacifist: Devere Allen and the Interwar Peace Movement, 1918–1940.* New York: Macmillan, 1980.

Anderson, Paul B. "Church and State in the Soviet Union," in *The Church and State,* edited by Kenneth G. Grubb, 239–264. London: Oxford University Press, 1939.

———. "The Legacy of John R. Mott," *Journal of Ecumenical Studies* 16 (1979), 27–30.

———. *No East or West.* Paris: YMCA Press, 1985.

———. "The Orthodox Church in Soviet Russia," *Foreign Affairs* 39 (1961), 299–311.

———. "Reflections on Religion in Russia, 1917–1967," in *Aspects of Religion in the Soviet Union,* edited by Richard H. Marshall, Jr., 11–33. Chicago, IL: University of Chicago Press, 1971.

Ashby, LeRoy. *Spearless Leader: Senator Borah and the Progressive Movement in the 1920s.* Urbana: University of Illinois Press, 1972.

Asquith, Michael. *Famine: Quaker Work in Russia, 1921–1923.* Oxford: Oxford University Press, 1943.

Baker, Christina Looper. *In a Generous Spirit: A First Person Biography of Myra Page.* Urbana: University of Illinois Press, 1996.

Ball, Alan M. *Imagining America: Influence and Images in Twentith Century Russia.* Lanham, MD: Rowman and Littlefield, 2003.

Barnes, Harper. *Standing on a Volcano: The Life and Times of David Towland Francis.* St. Louis: Missouri Historical Society, 2001.

Bassow, Whitman. *The Moscow Correspondents: Reporting on Russia from the Revolution to Glasnost.* New York: Paragon House, 1989.

Berdyaev, Nikolai. Ot redaktsii. "Dukhovnyia zadachi russkoi emigratsii," *Put',* No. 1 (September, 1925), 3–8.

"Beseda tov. Iaroslavskogo s amerikanskoi delegatsiei," *Bezbozhnik,* No. 17–18 (September, 1932), 5–6. Continuation in Nos. 19–20 (October 1932), 7.

Bohlen, Charles. *Witness to History, 1929–1969.* New York: Norton, 1973.

Bourke-White, Margaret. *Eyes on Russia.* New York: Simon and Schuster, 1931.

Bowers, Robert E. "Senator Arthur Robinson of Indiana Vindicaed: William Bullitt's Secret Mission to Europe," *Indiana Magazine of History* 41(Sepember, 1965), 189–204.

Brandenburg, Hans. *The Meek and the Mighty: The Emergence of the Evangelical Movement in Russia.* London: Mowbrays, 1976.

Brands, H. W. *Inside the Cold War: Loy Henderson and the Rise of the American Empire, 1918–1961.* New York: Oxford University Press, 1991.

Brooks, Jeffrey. "The Press and Its Message: Images of America in the 1920s and 1930s," in *Russia in the Era of NEP: Explorations in Soviet Society and Culture.* Bloomington: Indiana University Press, 1991.

Brooks, Jesse W., ed. *Good News for Russia.* Chicago, IL: The Bible Institute Colportage Association, 1918.

Bryant, Louise. *Mirrors of Moscow.* New York: Seltzer, 1923.

Bulgakov, Sergei. *A Bulgakov Anthology.* Edited by James Pain and Nicolas Zernov. Philadelphia, PA: Westminster Press, 1976.

Bullitt, William C. *It's Not Done.* New York: Harcourt Brace and Company, 1926.

Byrnes, Robert F. *Awakening American Education to the World: The Role of Archibald Cary Coolidge, 1866–1928.* Notre Dame, IN: University of Notre Dame Press, 1982.

Calian, Carnegie S. *Icon and Pulpit: The Protestant-Orthodox Encounter.* Philadelphia, PA: Westminster, 1968.

Cassella-Blackburn, Michael. *The Donkey, the Carrot, and the Club: William C. Bullitt and Soviet-American Relations, 1917–1948.* Westport, CN: Praeger, 2004.

Caute, David. *The Fellow Travellers: A Postscript to the Enlightenment.* New York: Macmillan, 1973.

Chatfield, Charles, ed. *Devere Allen: Life and Writings.* New York: Garland Publishing, 1976.

Chesterton, Mrs. Cecil. *My Russian Adventure.* Philadelphia, PA: Lippincott, 1931.

Coleman, Heather. *Russian Baptists and Spiritual Revolution: 1905–1929.* Bloomington: Indiana University Press, 2005.

Colton, Ethan T. "With the Y.M.C.A. in Revolutionary Russia," *The Russian Review* 14, No. 2 (April, 1955), 128–139.

Coolidge, Archibald Cary ["K"]. "Russia after Genoa and the Hague," *Foreign Affairs* 1, No. 1 (September, 1922), 133–155.

Dalrymple, Dana. "American Technology and Soviet Agricultural Development, 1924–1933," *Agricultural History* 40, No. 3 (July, 1966), 187–206.

Davis, Donald E. and Eugene P. Trani. "An American in Russia: Russell M. Story and the Bolshevik Revolution, 1917–1919," *The Historian* 36, No. 4 (August, 1974), 704–721.

Davis, Jerome. *A Life Adventure for Peace: An Autobiography.* New York: Citadel, 1967.

Dearborn, Mary V. *Queen of Bohemia: The Life of Louise Bryant.* Boston, MA: Houghton Mifflin, 1996.

Dewey, John. *Impressions of Soviet Russia and the Revolutionary World: Mexico-China-Turkey, 1929.* New York: New Republic, 1929.

Dexter, Byron. *The Years of Opportunity: The League of Nations, 1920–1926.* New York: Viking, 1967.

Diefenthaler, Jon. "H. Richard Niebuhr: A Lifetime of Reflections on the Church and the World," *Journal of American History* 74, No. 1 (June, 1987), 226–237.

Dorn, Harold. "Hugh Lincoln Cooper and the First Détente," *Technology and Culture* 20 (1979), 322–347.

Dreiser, Theodore. *Dreiser Looks at Russia.* New York: Liveright, 1928.

Dubie, Alain. *Frank A. Golder: An Adventure of a Historian in Quest of Russian History.* Boulder, CO: East European Monographs, 1989.

Dukes, Paul. "The Secret Door," *The Atlantic Monthly* 128 (July, 1921), 1–13.

Duncan, Isadora. *My Life.* New York: Boni and Liveright, 1927.

Eddy, Sherwood. *The Challenge of Russia.* New York: Farrar and Rinehart, 1931.

———. *Eighty Adventurous Years: An Autobiography.* New York: Harper and Brothers, 1955.

———. *A Pilgrimage of Ideas, or the Re-education of Sherwood Eddy.* New York: Farrar and Rinehart, 1934.

Eddy, Sherwood and Kirby Page. *Creative Pioneers.* New York: Association Press, 1937.

Eden, Anthony. *The Memoirs of Anthony Eden, Earl of Avon: Facing the Dictators, 1923–1938.* Boston, MA: Houghton Mifflin, 1962.

Ehrenburg, Ilya. *Memoirs: 1921–1941.* Translated by Tatania Shebunina. Cleveland, OH: World, 1964.

Engerman, David Charles. *Modernization from the Other Shore: American Intellectuals and the Romance of Russian Development.* Cambridge, MA: Harvard University Press, 2003.

Farnsworth, Beatrice. *William C. Bullitt and the Soviet Union.* Bloomington: Indiana University Press, 1967.

Farson, Negley. *Black Bread and Red Coffins.* New York: Century, 1930.

Fey, Harold E., ed. *Kirby Page, Social Evangelist: Autobiography of 20th Century Prophet for Peace.* Nyack, NY: Fellowship Press, 1975.

Filene, Peter G. *Americans and the Soviet Experiment, 1917–1933.* Cambridge, MA: Harvard University Press, 1967.

Fischer, Louis. *Machines and Men in Russia.* New York: Harrison Smith, 1932.

———. *Men and Politics: Europe between the Two World Wars.* New York: Harper Colophon, 1966.

———. *Soviet Journey.* New York: Harrison Smith and Robert Haas, 1935.

Fisher, Harold H. *The Famine in Soviet Russia, 1919–1923: The Operations of the American Relief Administration.* New York: Macmillan, 1927.

Fosdick, Harry Emerson. *The Living of These Days.* New York: Harper, 1956.

Fox, Richard W. "H. Richard Niebuhr's Divided Kingdom," *American Quarterly* 42, No. 1 (March, 1990), 93–101.

Friedheim, Robert F. *The Seattle General Strike* Seattle: University of Washington Press, 1964.

Goldman, Emma. *My Disillusionment in Russia.* Intro. By Rebecca West. New York: Thomas Y. Crowell (Apollo), 1950.

Gorsuch, Anne. *Flappers and Foxtrotters: Soviet Youth in the "Roaring Twenties,"* Carl Beck Papers, No. 1102. Pittsburgh, PA: University of Pittsburgh Press, 1994.

Grant, Natalie. "The Russian Section: A Window on the Soviet Union" *Diplomatic History* 2, No. 1 (Winter, 1978), 107–115.

Halle, Fannina W. *Woman in Soviet Russia.* London: Routledge, 1933.

Hapgood, Norman. *The Changing Years: Reminiscences of Norman Hapgood.* New York: Farrar and Rinehart, 1933.

Hardeman, Hilde. *Coming to Terms with the Soviet Regime: The "Changing Signposts" Movement among Russian Emigres in the early 1920s.* DeKalb: Northern Illinois University Press, 1994.

Harper, Samuel. *The Russia I Believed In: The Memoirs of Samuel N. Harpter, 1902–1941.* Edited by Paul Harpter. Chicago, IL: University of Chicago Press, 1945.

Harriman, Mrs. J. Borden. *From Pinafores to Politics.* New York: Henry Holt, 1923.

Harrington, Daniel F. "Kennan, Bohlen, and the Riga Axions," *Diplomatic History* 2, No. 4 (Fall, 1978), 423–437.

Harrison, Marguerite. *Marooned in Moscow: The Story of an American Woman Imprisoned in Russia.* New York: Doran, 1921.

Haywood, Harry. *Black Bolshevik: Autobiography of an Afro-American Communist.* Chicago, IL: Liberator Press, 1978.

Hecker, Julius F. *Religion and Communism: A Study of Religion and Atheism in Soviet Russia.* London: Chapman and Hall, 1933.

———. "The Russian Church under the Soviets," *Methodist Review* 107, No. 4 (July, 1924), 542–555.

Henderson, Loy. *A Question of Trust: The Origins of U.S. Soviet Relations – The Memoirs of Loy W. Henderson.* Edited by George W. Baer. Stanford, CA: Hoover Institution Press, 1986.

Hiebert, Peter Cornelius and Orie O. Miller. *Feeding the Hungry: Russia Famine, 1919–1925.* Scottsdale, PA: Mennonite Central Committee, 1929.

Hindus, Maurice. *Broken Earth.* London: T.J. Unwin, 1926.

———. *Humanity Uprooted.* New York: Cape and H. Smith, 1930.

———. *Red Bread.* New York: Jonathan Cape and Harrison Smith, 1931.

Hollander, Paul. *Political Pilgrims: Western Intellectuals in Search of the Good Society.* New Brunswick, NJ: Transaction Publishers, 1998.

Hughes, Langston. *I Wonder as I Wander: An Autobiographical Journey.* New York: Thunder's Mouth Press, 1986.

———. *Moscow and Me: A Noted American Writer Relates His Experiences.* Moscow: International Union of Revolutionary Writers, 1933.

Huntington, W. Chapin. *The Homesick Million: Russia-out-of-Russia.* Boston, MA: Stratford, 1933.

Ilyin, Olga. *White Road: A Russian Odyssey, 1919–1923.* New York: Holt, Rinehart and Winston, 1984.

Jacobson, Jon. *When the Soviet Union Entered World Politics.* Berkeley: University of California Press, 1994.

Jones, Rufus M. *A Service of Love in Wartime.* New York: Macmillan, 1920.

Kagedan, Allan L. "American Jews and the Soviet Experiment: The Agro-Joint Project, 1924–1937," *Jewish Social Studies* 43, No. 2 (1981), 153–164.

Karlowich, Robert A. "Stranger in a Far Land: Report of a Bookbuying Trip by Harry Miller Lydenberg in Eastern Europe and Russia in 1923–1924," *Bulletin of Research in the Humanities* 87, No. 1 (1986–1987), 182–224.

Kennell, Ruth Eperson. *Theodore Dreiser and the Soviet Union, 1927–1945: A First Hand Chonicle.* New York: International Publishers, 1969.

Killen, Linda. *The Russia Bureau: A Case Study in Wilsonian Diplomacy.* Lexington: University Press of Kentucky, 1983.

Lee, Ivy. *Present-Day Russia.* New York: MacMillan, 1928.

Leonard, Raymond W. *Secret Soldiers of the Revooution: Soviet Military Intelligence, 1918–1933.* Westport, CT: Greenwood Press, 1999.

Levine, Issac Don. *Eyewitness to History: Memoirs and Reflections of a Foreign Correspondent for Half a Century.* New York: Hawthorne Books, 1973.

Lindenmeyr, Adele. *Poverty Is Not a Vice: Charity, Society, and the State in Imperial Russia.* Princeton, NJ: Princeton University Press, 1996.

Lindberg, Anne Morrow. *North to the Orient.* New York: Harcourt Brace, 1935.

Long, James W. *From Privileged to Dispossessed: The Volga Germans, 1860–1917.* Lincoln: University of Nebraska Press, 1988.

Long, Ray. *An Editor Looks at Russia: One Unprejudiced View of the Land of the Soviets.* New York: Ray Long and Richard Smith, 1931.

Lowrie, Donald A. *The Light of Russia: An Introduction to the Russian Church.* Prague: YMCA Press, 1923.

Mackenzie. F. A. *Russia before Dawn.* London: T. Fisher Unwin, 1923.

Macmillan, Margaret. *Paris 1919: Six Months that Changed the World.* New York: Random House, 2002.

Margulies, Sylvia. *The Pilgrimage to Russia: the Soviet Union and the Treatment of Foreigners, 1924–1937.* Madison: University of Wisconsin Press, 1968.

Marks, StevenG. *How Russia Shaped the Modern World: From Art to Anti-Semitism, Ballet to Bolshevism.* Princeton, NJ: Princeton University Press, 2003.

McCown, Chester. *The Genesis of the Social Gospel.* New York and London: Alfred A. Knopf, 1929.

McCullagh, Francis. *A Prisoner of the Reds: The Story of a British Officer Captured in Siberia.* New York: E.P. Dutton, 1922.

McDaniel, George William. *Smith Wildman Brookhart: Iowa's Renegade Republican.* Ames: Iowa State University Press, 1995.

McKay, Claude. *A Long Way from Home.* New York: Lee, Furman, 1937.

McKenna, Kevin J. *All the Views Fit to Print: Changing Images of the U.S. in Pravda Political Cartoons, 1917–1991.* New York: Peter Lang, 2001.

McVay, Gordon. *Esenin: A Life.* New York: Paragon, 1988.

Moen, Lars. *Are You Going to Russia?* London: Chapman and Hall, 1934.

Monkhouse, Allan. *Moscow, 1911–1933: Being the Memoirs of Allan Monkhouse.* London: Victor Gillancz, 1933.

Moore, David Chioni. "Colored Dispatches from the Uzbek Border: Langston Hughes' Relevance, 1933–2002," *Callaloo* 25, 4 (Fall, 2002), 1115–1135.

Mott, John R. *Addresses and Papers of John R. Mott. Vol. 3, The Young Men's Christian Association.* New York: Association Press, 1947.

Niebuhr, H. Richard. *Theology, History, and Culture: Major Unpublished Writings*. New Haven, CT: Yale, 1996.

Nutt, Rick L. *The Whole Gospel for the Whole World: Sherwood Eddy and the American Protestant Mission* Macon, GA: Mercer University Press, 1997.

O'Connor, Timothy Edward. *Diplomacy and Revolution: G.V. Chicherin and Soviet Foreign Affairs, 1918–1930*. Ames: Iowa State University Press, 1988.

———. *The Engineer of Revolution: L.B. Krasin and the Bolsheviks, 1870–1926*. Boulder, CO: Westview, 1992.

Page, Dorothy Myra. *Gathering Storm*. Moscow: International Publishers, 1932

Page, Kirby. *Christianity and Economic Problems*. New York, 1922.

———. *Jesus or Christianity*. New York, 1929.

———. *Kirby Page, Social Evangelist: The Autobiography of a 20th Century Prophet for Peace*. New York: Fellowship Press, 1975.

Patenaude, Bertrand M. *The Big Show in Bololand: The American Relief Expedition to Soviet Russia in the Famine of 1921*. Stanford, CA: Stanford University Press, 2002.

Phillips, Hugh D. *Between the Revolution and the West: A Political Biography of Maxim M. Lirtvinov*. Boulder, CO: Westview, 1992.

Raeff, Marc. *Russia Abroad: A Cultural History of the Russian Emigration, 1919–1939*. New York: Oxford University Press, 1990.

Raleigh, Donald J. *Experiencing Russia's Civil War: Politics, Society, and Revolutionary Culture in Saratov, 1917–1923*. Princeton, NJ: Princeton University Press, 2002.

Remple, Henry D. *From Bolshevik Russia to America: A Mennonite Family Story*. Sioux Falls, SD: Pine Hill Press, 2001.

Roslof, Edward E. *Red Priests: Renovationism, Russian Orthodoxy, and Revolution, 1905–1946*. Bloomington: Indiana University Press, 2002.

Salzman, Neil. *Reform and Revolution: The Life and Times of Raymond Robins*. Kent, OH: Kent State University Press, 1991.

Schmidt, Regin. *Red Scare: RbI and the Origins of Anticommunism in the United States, 1919–1943*. Copenhagen: University of Copenhagen, 2000.

Sheinis, Zinovy. *Maxim Litvinov*. Translated by Vic Schneierson. Moscow, Progress, 1990.

Shragin, Boris and Albert Todd, eds. *Landmarks: A Collection of Essays on the Russian Intelligentsia, 1909. Berdyaev, Bulgakov, Gershenzon, Izgoev, Kistyakovsky, Struve, Frank*. New York: Karz Howard, 1977.

Sinclair, Upton. *The Autobiography of Upton Sinclair*. New York: Harcourt, Brace, 1962.

Sorokin, Pitirim A. *A Long Journey: the Autobiography of Pitirim Sorokin*. New Haven, CT: College and University Press, 1963.

Sparks, Nemmy and Ruth Epperson Kennel. "Americans at Kuzbas, 1922–1924," *New World Review* 39 (Fall, 1971), 68–98.

Steffens, Lincoln. *The Autobiography of Lincoln Steffens*. New York: Harcourt, Brace, 1931.

Steinberg, Mark D. *Proletarian Imagination: Self, Modernity, and the Sacred in Russia, 1910–1925.* Ithaca, NY: Cornell University Press, 2002.

Steuer, Kenneth Andrew. *Pursuit of an "Unparalleled Opportunity": The American YMCA and Prisoner-of-War Diplomacy among the Central Power Nations during World War I, 1914–1923.* New York: Columbia University Press, 2009.

Strong, Anna Louise. *Children of Revolution: Story of the John Reed Children's Colony on the Volga.* Seattle, WA: Pigott, 1926.

———. *I Change Worlds: The Remaking of an American.* New York: Garden City Publishing Company, 1937.

Tsikhilashvili, Nana Sh. and David Ch. Engerman. "Amerikanskaia pomoshch' Roissii v 1921–1923 godakh: konflikty I sotrushnechestov," *Amerikanskii Ezhegodnik* (1995), 191–213.

Von Mohrenschildt, Dmitri. "The Early American Observers of the Russian Revolution, 1917–1921," *Russian Review* 3 (1943), 64–74.

Walsh, Warren B., ed. "Documents: Petrograd, March-July 1917: The Letters of Edward T. Heald," *The American Slavic and East European Review* 6, Nos. 16–17 (May, 1947), 116–157.

White, William Allen. *The Autobiography of William Allen White.* New York: Macmillan, 1946.

———. *Woodrow Wilson: The Man, His Times, His Tasks.* Boston, MA: Houghton Mifflin, 1924.

Yakobson, Helen. *Crossing Borders: From Revolutionary Russia to China to America.* Tenafly, NJ: Hermitage, 1994.

Youngbloos, Denise. *Movies for the Masses: Popular Cinema and Soviet Society in the 1920s.* Cambridge, MA: Cambridge University Press, 1992.

Zatko, James J. "The Vatican and Famine Relief in Russia," *Slavonic and East European Review* 42 (1963), 54–63.

Index